Praise fo

"*I See You* will deeply impact any woman who may be exhausted yet still yearns for more. Amy Kemp deftly teaches us that by thinking differently, we can create a tremendous amount of success and wealth without struggle or strain. This book is truly a game changer."

BARBARA HUSON, author of *Overcoming Underearning* and *Rewire for Wealth*

"*I See You* grounds professional guidance in a deep understanding of what it feels like to be in our big, beautiful, and sometimes messy and stressful lives. Amy Kemp delivers just the right balance of advice and encouragement, helping us to not only love the life we are in, but to accomplish our wildest dreams."

PAMELA SLIM, author of *Body of Work* and *The Widest Net*

"In *I See You*, Amy Kemp uncovers the resistance you face in constructing support structures and gives you the fix. You're about to conquer the trap of poor thinking habits and start seeing the results you deserve."

MIKE MICHALOWICZ, author of *All In* and *Profit First*

"Amy Kemp has cracked the code for hard-working, family-focused leaders who haven't yet achieved the results they want and deserve. In *I See You*, she illuminates the thought habits that keep us from our dreams and offers simple yet powerful thinking shifts to create the life we want."

AJ HARPER, award-winning author of *Write a Must-Read*

"Every once in a while we get the opportunity to read one of *those* books—one in which the author masterfully and authentically lets you in their world, one in which the author shares real-life experiences and wisdom so badly needed today by powerful yet often confused women. I have four daughters. Each one is receiving a copy of this book."

DAVE BLANCHARD, author of *Today I Begin a New Life*, *The Observer's Chair*, and *Equanimity*

"*I See You* is more than a book of quick-fix strategies that you've read a hundred times; it's a guide to real, lasting life-change for women. After reading it, I believe more than ever that we don't have to work more to get what we want."

TAMSEN WEBSTER, designer and author of *Find Your Red Thread*

"Amy Kemp has given all women a unique and valuable gift with *I See You*. This is not an amateur's attempt to give some quick tips and strategies; this book offers an intimate, empathic journey, and it will change the personal and professional lives of so many readers."

DOUG MCKINLEY, host of *Leadership Currency* and author of *The Resiliency Quest*

"I first met Amy Kemp in South America on a quest to hike to the ancient fortress of Machu Picchu. Over days of hiking, I came to learn she's not afraid of a challenge and she's an encourager who is determined to get the entire team to their destination. I love how she has compiled her wisdom and energy into this book. I found myself scribbling lots of notes as I read *I See You*. You're gonna love this book!"

JOËL MALM, founder of Summit Leaders and author of *Connecting the Dots*

I
SEE
YOU

AMY KEMP

SEE

A Guide for Women
to Make More, Have More,
and Be More—
Without More Work

YOU

Cataloguing in publication information is
available from Library and Archives Canada.
ISBN 978-1-77458-442-2 (paperback)
ISBN 978-1-77458-443-9 (ebook)

Page Two
pagetwo.com

Edited by Emily Schultz
Copyedited by Rachel Ironstone
Proofread by Crissy Boylan
Cover and interior design by Taysia Louie
Cover photo by Sarah Jane Photography

AmyKemp.com

*To every woman who has bravely trusted me
to guide and lead them over the past
twenty-five years and whose incredible stories
of transformation have filled this book,
this is for you.*

I see you.

Contents

Introduction

FOR MORE than twenty years, the mission of my work has been the development and support of women. A recent conversation I had with a local female leader reminded me why this targeted investment in women is so needed. It also reinforced the purpose of this book and inspired the title. Allow me to share more about this brief, fated interaction.

A mutual friend introduced me to this leader at a local networking event, and I sincerely enjoyed the brief conversation she and I shared, so I reached out and invited her to join me for a cup of coffee—my treat! For about an hour, she shared with me all about her professional and personal journey, which was filled with impressive accolades and accomplishments. Her decisions impact the lives of hundreds of people every day, she has a seat at some tables that have a significant influence on the health and future of our community, and she mixes all of her professional responsibilities in with a busy family life as well. From the outside, this woman has it all together.

After sharing her story, she looked me straight in the eye, and with a touch of skepticism, she asked me why I had invited her for coffee. I met her gaze straight on and said the first words that came to my mind: "Because I see you. I really *see* you."

She put her face in her hands right in the middle of that busy coffee shop and silently but sincerely wept... for what felt like a *long* time. I let her. She very obviously needed it. When she finally paused and caught her breath, she looked up at me, wiped her eyes with the back of her hand, and said, "So few people do. Thank you."

I know. That's why I wrote this book. It is not a book full of quick tips and strategies. I am not here in a position of authority, swooping in to impart my sage wisdom upon you; in fact, I'm not even here to position myself as the expert teacher and you as the student. You are all experts in your own right, even if you don't know it yet. (Spoiler alert: helping you understand how astonishingly brilliant you are is one of my biggest goals in the coming pages!)

Women like you and this new friend I met for coffee don't need a complete system overhaul. You may need some updates to the way you think, which we will work through together, but more than anything, you need to know that someone *sees* you... someone sees *all* of you.

As you read, I hope you feel like you are sitting in an intimate one-on-one coaching session with me. I am your personal guide, humbled and honored to be along for the journey. Throughout the book, you will read about a concept and then be prompted to respond in exercises at the end of each chapter. Don't skip these! There's no secret you need to rush to find in the pages ahead. Most of what you need is already inside you; you just need to uncover it. These exercises are your tools to do the important excavation work.

More than anything, I know that your families, your places of work and businesses, your communities, and our entire *world* need you at your best. When women are healthy and confident, everyone wins.

1

A Moment of Truth

O N A late afternoon in August of 2017, my husband, Ryan, and I sat side by side in matching maroon burlap chairs in the air-conditioned office of our trusted financial advisor, Tess. I had spent several hours preparing for the meeting, filling out forms that painted a clear picture of our current financial status. Everything there was to know about our money was covered in detail in the forms: income; current investments; college, retirement, and liquid savings; real estate; and a detailed outline of our family budget. Ryan and I had also discussed and filled out a questionnaire that helped us define and clarify our future goals. We answered questions like, Do you want to pay for your children's college education? How much money do you want to have to live on when you retire? How old do you want to be when you retire?

Tess leaned forward onto her arms on top of her desk, with all the forms neatly stacked in front of her. In a kind, sincere voice, she said, "I've reviewed everything, and I'm so impressed with how organized you are—even with your budget. You certainly aren't overspending, and you know where every penny of your money is going. There's only one problem if you want to achieve your goals, particularly paying for college for all three of your kids." She paused for what seemed like a long time and then said, "You're not making enough money."

It felt like all the air left the room.

She went on to explain that we could always adjust our goals. Perhaps we could pay for only a portion of college for the kids; we could adjust our goals by pushing back the age at which we would have the option of retiring or by deciding to live on less in our retirement years. But after that one sentence, her words all blended together like the muffled, undecipherable murmurs of Charlie Brown's teacher: "Wah, wah-wah, wah, wahhh." I couldn't digest anything else because my entire world had shifted with that one simple, piercingly true statement.

"You're not making enough money."

At first, I felt so ashamed and frustrated. For fifteen years, I had built a business in direct sales. I was leading a thriving, growing organization of successful independent sales consultants. I got lots of recognition and prizes, earned amazing incentive trips to exotic locations around the world, had the use of a free luxury vehicle, and I had frequent opportunities to teach and speak at important company events. The salesforce and corporate staff of the company looked to me for direction and feedback. I had sincerely poured my heart and soul into the people I led in my organization. I had also taken thousands and thousands of the tiny daily steps of growing a business that aren't glamorous but that add up to significant results: consistently holding appointments, building my client base through referrals and networking, leading weekly sales meetings, communicating on a regular basis about promotions and products, and coaching up-and-coming leaders. However, in spite of all my work and dedication and in spite of the public perceptions of my success, after all of my business expenses and taxes, there just wasn't enough money left over to achieve our goals. That was a difficult reality to digest.

Our three kids were in grade school and high school, and all three were in their busiest seasons of travel and school sports. Most nights, Ryan and I fell into bed, exhausted after managing a flurry of practices, family dinners, meetings, and games, catching some quick sleep so we could wake and do it all again the next day. Ryan was an assistant principal and athletic director at a local high school. He spent his days at school handling student discipline issues and making sure the operations of the building ran smoothly. In the evening, his schedule was slammed with all of our kids' activities plus the supervision of a variety of high school events. While his job provided great insurance and retirement benefits, the only way he could get a pay raise was to get older. Even then, the annual increase was relatively small. In addition, his packed schedule would not allow him to take on any more work.

As Tess continued to talk, I quickly scanned her office, desperately searching for anyone in the room who could rescue me from the weight of the responsibility that had just descended on my shoulders. This was *my* problem to solve? Really? It didn't take long to confirm that I was, in fact, the *only* one left in the room who could take on this problem. I was the one whose income was variable, changing based on sales and monthly commission checks from my business. I was the one who had the most opportunity to earn more. I was the one whose schedule could change without permission from anyone else. And even though the weight of providing for our family felt heavy in that moment, I knew right then that something had to change. Actually, to be more precise, *someone* had to change. And that someone was me.

Quitting isn't always failure; sometimes it is the most needed next step to growth.

This Is Me

I am by most accounts a pretty straitlaced person. I don't drink. I don't smoke. Outside of an occasional Netflix binge, I don't have many vices... but if I have one addiction, it would be to my work. Yes, work can be an addiction, and if you picked up this book, maybe it's an issue you grapple with as well. My default when faced with most challenges is to simply put my head down and work more hours. I knew from years of experience in sales that under the pressure of a goal with a clear purpose and deadline, very few people would or could outwork me.

However, this default of working *more* comes at a cost. It requires a great deal of time and emotional energy, and already I had increased the number of hours and the intensity of my work to maximum capacity. At home, my investment in my kids' lives at this particular season felt more crucial and finite than it had at any other time. I wasn't willing to miss games and family events or, more importantly, the conversations that happened in between all those daily experiences. Whatever changes I made could not require any more energy or time from me. There wasn't any more to give.

Over the next few months, the initial shock and shame I felt at that meeting with Tess was replaced with a firm and unwavering decision: we would *not* change the financial goals we had set for our family. That was not an option. I didn't know what I was going to do, but I was going to create the income we needed.

As this realization settled in, a steady stream of questions filled my mind.

- If I'm already exhausted by my work and life outside of work, where will I find the energy to create something new?

- If my current leadership responsibilities already feel draining, why would I want to lead more people?

- Is it even possible to increase my income without sacrificing the time and energy that I want to devote to my family and other priorities outside of work?

- How much longer can I keep working at this pace?

- What do I need to *do* to get to the next level of income, influence, and impact? And if it's not something I need to do, how do I become more? What are the practical steps for *that*?

- Most people already see me as exceedingly successful. What will they think of me if I achieve this new level of success? Will I be too much for them? Will this shift negatively impact important relationships in my life?

And perhaps most painful of all:

- What is wrong with me that I haven't been able to figure this out? I've worked so hard and for so long and still haven't produced enough.

Change Is in the Air

Over the next few years, I grappled with these questions and all of the emotions that accompanied them. With the guidance and patient help of several important coaches and mentors, I discovered that any changes I made in my work or behavior would be fleeting if I didn't get down to the roots of the thought habits driving my choices.

More than anything, I learned that I could not outwork my thought habits. Instead of just putting my head down and pushing harder like I always had before, I had to first uproot the unhealthy thought habits that were so deeply buried I hadn't even realized they were there. After working with ambitious women for more than two decades, I know that these habits of thinking are not unique to my experience. Women everywhere of all ages, ethnicities, and levels of experience battle them. Perhaps you will be able to relate to some of the loudest noise that filled my head.

My thought habits wanted me to believe the only way to earn more money was to work more hours and sacrifice my own well-being. I hear this fear expressed frequently by women who don't pursue a promotion or opportunity to earn more income because they don't want to add more time commitments to an already overloaded schedule. I also felt deeply responsible for the success or failure of those I was leading; therefore, transitioning into a new business felt selfish and harmful to those who I was leaving.

At times, my habits of thinking kept me tethered to outdated, counterproductive groupthink that was just creating more of what I already had. One of the most pervasive messages I had to leave behind in order to move forward said, "You can only be a failure if you quit." Actually, in order to move forward, the *first step was to quit*! I quit doing work that wasn't paying me what I was worth. I quit giving away my intellectual property and valuable training for free. I quit believing that there was only one way to fulfill my purpose in life and opened myself up to other possibilities. Quitting isn't always failure; sometimes it is the most needed next step.

The thoughts in my head were persistent, incessant. They taunted me with warnings about what other people would think if I took a different path, and they told me I should just be satisfied with what I had. After all, it was more than most. Sometimes, these thoughts could even sneakily convince me that my ambition was selfish or that wanting more was a fatal flaw or a spiritual death spiral. I had many real-life conversations with well-meaning but critical people who did have opinions about the choices I was making as I transitioned professionally. After hearing about my new coaching business, an acquaintance I ran into at a local event asked me with a tone of sincere concern in her voice, "When will it be enough, Amy? Will you ever be satisfied? You're already the queen of everything in your company." While I won't lie and say these words didn't cut deeply, I decided that my ambition is actually one of the most compelling, beautiful parts of me. I also realized that everyone will have an opinion about the choices I make, and this is true no matter what I do. Some will agree with my choices; some will be harsh and judgmental. Others' responses can provide information that *I get to decide* to consider or toss. Their feedback truly says more about the people offering it than it does about me.

As I took bold steps in a new direction, I set boundaries that felt so scary they took my breath away. Some of those boundaries resulted in losing relationships that I still grieve today. I spent more time doing the things that felt so easy to me and that consistently astonished people around me, and while at first it felt uncomfortable, I started charging people for these things instead of giving them away for free. I started taking back the power I had given away to other people and let go of feeling responsible for everyone else's success. I embraced business-building structures that created more profit, and with each tiny step, I started to forget about others' opinions. I became so engrossed in creating and growing my business, my need for external approval quietly dissipated.

Probably the most important step I took along the way was in December of 2017, when I officially opened the doors of my coaching business. The birth of this business was quite unexpected, even to me, without the hint of a long-term strategic plan.

I was speaking at an event in Park City, Utah, and I reached out to one of my former business coaches, who lived in Salt Lake City, to let him know I would be in town. We had stayed in touch after our years of working together, and I always loved reconnecting with him when I had a chance. He picked me up from the airport, and over dinner I told him all about my commitment to increase my earnings and that I had simultaneously started having this deep feeling that I was supposed to start working with women outside the context of my other business. Everywhere I turned, this gut feeling had been confirmed. I'd listen to a podcast, and the message would urge me to take action on the idea. I'd have lunch with a friend, and she'd encourage me to get going. I'd flip open the pages of a new personal development book, and the words would confirm that I needed to move forward.

At the same time, without even trying, I *constantly* found myself having deep, meaningful conversations with women who were leading businesses or organizations in our community. These conversations were full of similar themes: isolation, self-doubt, exhaustion, frustration, and overwhelm at the demands of work and home responsibilities. I knew that if I could somehow gather these women together, they would see that they were not alone and, within the context of a small, safe community, they could all grow together.

Upon hearing this, without a moment's hesitation, my coach said, "We are starting training for new coaches who want to use the assessment tool and curriculum I do on Monday. You could always jump in and use it to help these women. I really think you need to turn this idea into reality."

Until that moment, coaching people using the tools we had used in our engagement had never occurred to me. But without question, what was plaguing all of these women I knew was the same thing I had discovered was holding me back—limiting thought habits. The coaching experience I had received changed my own life and business more than any other personal development experience I had invested in throughout my career. Because it was so far from my own idea, and in spite of having only four days to decide whether I would jump into the training, it made *perfect* sense to me.

I talked the idea, and the significant financial investment in the training, over with my husband, Ryan, who simply said, "Every time we've invested in you, it has been more than worth it. You should do it." (Can we all pause for a moment and be overwhelmingly grateful for healthy, supportive spouses? I am beyond thankful for Ryan's constant, unwavering belief in me.) Four days later, I started the training, and I officially created a new corporation a week later to house this new business.

Where I've Landed

What has transpired over the last five years has exceeded my wildest expectations. I'm so grateful I *didn't* have a well-thought-out strategic plan when it all started, because I'm confident I would have sold myself incredibly short. Today, I work with clients in one-on-one engagements I call Empower, where we dive deeply into their habits of thinking in one-hour sessions every other week. I lead small groups of women who live all around the United States through a four-month experience called Encounter, in which we identify and start to replace limiting habits of thinking together in biweekly lunch meetings. I also lead two in-person experiences, called Pause and Refresh, that are crafted to serve women in meaningful, unique ways. Last but not least, I teach two online

You can't outwork your thought habits. If you could, you would have done it already.

webinars on a chosen topic each year—one in the fall and one in the spring.

Best of all, as I have applied my coaching principles to my own thought habits, I've tripled my income while working fewer hours than I ever have in my entire life. We are now talking with our financial advisor Tess about the progress we are making on the goals that were out of reach just a few years ago, and we are taking our investment strategies to the next level as our income continues to grow. Hundreds of women have "graduated" from my Encounter group coaching experience, and I have a full slate of one-on-one Empower clients who are experiencing the same results I have. One of these clients recently sent me an email full of gratitude as she had her best business month ever while also spending two weeks vacationing on a beach in February. She wrote, "You told me I could work fewer hours and earn more income when we started our coaching engagement, and I must confess I didn't believe you. I'm pinching myself today as I *live* it. Off to the sunshine and pool for the day! Thank you!"

Perhaps most important for you, my reader, is that the changes I've made have given me the freedom to finally get this book out of my brain and onto paper. I wrote it for you, an ambitious woman who is willing to work hard to grow a business or to advance her career but for whom the demands of life outside of work are significant. You want to grow and increase your levels of influence, impact, and income, but you don't have any more time or energy to give—you simply cannot work any harder or any longer.

You can't outwork your thought habits.

If you could, you would have done it already.

The next place you want to go personally or professionally requires that you dig deeper, not just travel farther. It requires that you show up differently, communicate with more clarity and confidence, and that you believe you are worth the level of influence and income these changes will create. It may ask that you work fewer hours (gasp) and that your work during those hours looks completely different than it has for the last stretch of your career. You may need to create some new boundaries, challenge the stories you are telling yourself, and learn how to connect with people more accurately, but you cannot continue to do more of the same and expect a different result.

You can't outwork your thought habits.

I offer no quick fixes or promises of instant transformation. The message I have for you *does* create change, but the process is slow. It is also lasting, and it is real. It may include being honest and uncomfortable and vulnerable. I can promise that you won't be alone on this journey. I'm here to guide you each step of the way. When you finish this book, I hope you realize that what you're looking for doesn't require working any longer or any harder or sacrificing more of *you* in the name of progress. Becoming more is the process of discovering that what you are searching for has been deep inside you all along.

CHAPTER 1 EXERCISE
AWARENESS IS THE FIRST STEP

Pull out your journal or meet with a trusted mentor or coach and spend some time answering these questions.

- What is it that you want or need to create most right now—more income, influence, impact? Perhaps you need a better quality of life or more time to devote to family and life outside of work?

- What resistance comes up if you are told that creating what you want most doesn't have to require more work? Be sure to jot these down—the first step to change your habits of thinking is identifying and observing them!

- What will happen if you don't change anything and keep living and working as you are for the next five, ten, even twenty years? Are there any repercussions or long-term consequences?

2

Leverage the Value
of Your Natural Genius

MOST WOMEN undervalue or can't easily identify their natural genius. I'm not sure why, but I see it again and again. Maybe it's because the places where we shine feel so easy to us, so we assume those skills are easy for everyone else too. In addition, women are culturally conditioned, especially in their relationships with other women, to not stand out too much. Most of us learn at a young age that showing off or bragging results in exclusion from desirable peer groups, and we take this to the extreme, downplaying our strengths for fear of rejection.

I'd love to illustrate this phenomenon with a story about a client I'll call Nicole. Nicole took over running the finances of a fledgling family business about sixteen years ago. The company opened right before the recession of 2008 hit. With her brilliant, strategic business mind at the helm as the CFO, the company not only navigated the challenges of getting off the ground in the middle of an economic downturn, but it has become the largest independently owned company in its industry in the Midwestern United States.

We were at a business event together recently, and I overheard her describing her role in the company to someone she had just met. She so vastly undersold herself in her description in this conversation, I would have thought her role was to balance the checkbook for a small mom and pop shop. To be clear: Nicole manages the finances of a growing multimillion-dollar company that is ten times larger than it was when she started! I was flabbergasted.

Here's the problem. This work feels easy to Nicole because it is in an area of natural genius for her. Combine this with the cultural conditioning that teaches women to stay small and not "brag" about our accomplishments, and we consistently and vastly undersell ourselves in spaces where we would benefit from a more accurate description of our accomplishments. I later told her that she should hear how *I* describe her when I tell others about her work and professional successes. Some might think we were talking about two very different people! I'm afraid women everywhere are doing this same thing and missing important connections and opportunities as a result.

This is why I spend a significant amount of time with my clients helping them identify and leverage their areas of natural genius more fully. In other words, I want you to do *a lot* of the thing that feels easy to you but astonishes everyone else. And I want you to get paid really well for doing it! *Everyone* has something they do that causes the people around them to exclaim, "How do you do that?!" And when people say that to you, inside, silently, you pause and think, "Uh ... it's not that hard. You just do it." *This* is your natural genius.

Let me give you a few examples of my own. Several years ago, a peer of mine who was running the same kind of business I was asked if she could drive to my office to see how I organized my supplies. Oh, and it was a two-hour drive! I agreed to her visit, thinking to myself, "Why in the world would she want to come and look at my office? Surely everyone must have a similar setup and systems in their offices. This trip is going to be a complete waste of time for her."

She arrived that day, eager and excited with a notebook in hand. I started to show her the office, not even really sure what she wanted to see. She walked around in a state of awe that morning, taking pictures of *everything*, as if she were seeing one of the Seven Wonders of the World. To my great amusement, she was especially captivated by the labels I had on the Rubbermaid shoeboxes tucked in the top shelf of my closet that held samples, ribbons, smaller boxes, and art supplies.

Inside my head, I have to confess I was laughing a little, thinking, "Really, you can't figure out what to label your Rubbermaid containers? You are a brilliant business owner and leader, and you are captivated by boxes with labels on them?" For whatever reason, creating simple organizational systems in an office or home comes as second nature to me. I don't even really have to think much about it. I learned that day in my office that this wasn't as easy for everyone as it was for me.

Everyone has different gifts and skills. We do what we are best at so easily we don't recognize how rare our skills are. These are our areas of natural genius, our places to shine! Let me give you some more examples.

A Barn Is Not Just Made of Wood

I worked one-on-one with a client, Angie, to harness her natural genius to make one of her dreams a reality. She wanted to transform an old run-down building on her rural property into a blend of a conference center, apartment, and multipurpose room to use for her business meetings, some ministries she supports, and for other fun community events. For decades, Angie's corporate job was in project management. In this role, she created a step-by-step plan for implementing changes in complex manufacturing and distribution processes and then led people through the implementation of those systems. I challenged her to use those same skills with her barn transformation project.

Not even an hour after our coaching call ended, Angie sent me a picture of a posterboard she had created that was covered with different colored Post-it Notes in a trail from the top to the bottom that looked like the path on the popular board game Candy Land. When I zoomed in to read what she had written, the first note in the upper left-hand corner of the posterboard made me laugh out loud. This note, describing the starting point of the project, simply said, "Barn that looks like a crack house." Well, I suppose it's good to acknowledge your starting point with complete clarity!

From that starting note, each piece of paper had words on it that described every step needed to transform that barn into the vision Angie had. One said, "Pick out cabinets." Then, the next, "Pick out tile and flooring." Step by step, she laid out a plan until the final Post-it Note at the bottom of the board: "Grand Opening!" As she made progress on the project, she covered each yellow sticky note with a green one. Step by step, day by day, and month by month, she focused on the next step until she had a finished barn, full of people she loves and leads.

Here's what is important about this story. Angie whipped up that Post-it Note poster with thirty steps to a finished barn in less than an hour. I think most people, myself included, wouldn't even know how to start *thinking* through a project of this scope, much less be able to come up with a color-coded system of implementation in less than sixty minutes. When I told her how amazing her posterboard was, Angie didn't think it was that uncommon or particularly brilliant. That's because this is her area of natural genius that causes her to think, "Duh, everyone can do this! It's not very hard." Everyone else looks at the process she created and says, "Whoa! That's so amazing! I could never do that!"

Coffee Beans and Human Beans

Here is another example of natural genius. I live about fifty miles south of Chicago in a suburban-ish town. About three miles from my house, you can find what I think is the best Starbucks in the entire world. It isn't the best because of its location; I've been inside much more aesthetically pleasing Starbucks shops than this one, and it offers the same menu of delightful food and drinks as every other Starbucks. But trust me, this Starbucks is different, and let me tell you why.

It's because of Justin. Justin, the manager at our amazing store, has become a friend to me over the last five years. When you walk into Justin's Starbucks and he is there, the entire space has a different vibe. It's upbeat, *packed* with people (as are many Starbucks), but the energy of this space is unique. Immediately, you feel welcomed and *known*.

One day, after I had been working there at a table for a couple of hours, I watched Justin leave after his shift ended. He talked to every single employee personally on his way out. "Good luck on your test tomorrow!" he said as he walked past one college-aged employee. "I hope your grandpa is feeling better!" he said to another man who works the drive-through like a beast. To another barista, he said, "Thanks for your hard work today!" And *then* he took off his apron, put on his coat, and stopped to say goodbye to about eight more people before getting out the door and in his car. He didn't stop at those tables because he was working or because it was mandated by Starbucks. He stopped just because that is who he is! Connecting with people and creating warm, inviting spaces are his natural genius.

Justin and the store were recently recognized at the national Starbucks leadership event. The sign on the enormous overhead banner at the event read: "Walking in the store you feel the energy and hear the baristas recognizing the customers by name before they get to the POS [point of sale]. This store is the true meaning of a community store." Justin isn't *trying* to be the way he is. He just is. It's his area of natural genius. Starbucks has leveraged his abilities, and their business is benefitting greatly from the warm, welcoming atmosphere he has created. It's his genius, his gift. We *all* have these abilities, and few of us recognize them in ourselves or value them highly enough.

My Genius Is Identifying the Genius in Others

Here's another example. Jennifer was one of my students when I was a high school English teacher, and while no good teacher should publicly admit they have a favorite student, I've been out of the traditional classroom long enough that it's safe to tell you that she was undoubtedly mine! After watching her work ethic and attention to detail in my classroom as a junior in high school, I hired her to be my office assistant when I started my first business. We have traveled through life together closely over the past twenty years since, and there is not much Jen doesn't know about me. She's seen me in many different stages of life, very up close and personal,

We tend to not recognize what our areas of genius are worth because they come so easily to us.

first as an office assistant and then while she handled all of our home and business bookkeeping for years after she graduated from college with her accounting degree.

Jen once said something to me that really resonated. She said, "I've realized over the years that you're not really *really* good at many things, but you are *great* at finding people who are really good at things and letting them help you." After I stopped laughing, I wrote down what she said because I had never recognized this in myself. She's right. I am great at finding talented people to do the things I'm not great at, and then I'm great at stepping back and letting them take care of me!

Over the years, as my businesses and our family has grown, I have used this unique gift to create a team of support people who have allowed me to work in *my* areas of genius, not wasting precious time or energy on things that aren't. I have incredibly talented, amazing people in these roles, and for that, I am eternally thankful. While there is an entire chapter about getting more help coming later in the book, I also want to share with you the list of these people so that you can see how much support I have running our home and my businesses. I am not doing this alone, and you don't have to either.

First, I have a college student who comes once a week to cook, do laundry, iron, and to do other random organizational projects in our home. I have someone who regularly cleans our house and changes the sheets on all the beds. I also have an exceptional office assistant who does all sorts of business-related tasks, such as data entry, sending monthly mailers, and managing systematic communication on social media and email. She helps service my clients by scheduling appointments, answering their questions about payment plans, and assisting with anything else they may need. In addition, she does a lot of personal work for me, returning all the clothes I buy online that don't fit, figuring out why we keep getting letters saying I didn't pay a toll when I clearly have a working transponder on the dash of my car (so annoying), taking clothes that don't fit or that we no longer wear to the consignment shop, and so much more.

Then I have a whole team of people outside of my home, most who work virtually, and many of whom even live in different states. I have two people who work with me on our finances: accounting, bookkeeping, bill paying, budget tracking, and QuickBooks. I have a graphic design person who designs promotional materials, newsletters, handouts for my online courses and workshops, and anything else I dream up that I want to look pretty. I have an amazing business manager who takes care of my CRM (customer relationship management software), helps me strategize for upcoming offerings and schedules, and creates campaigns to promote them. Curtis is my tech support person, and he runs all video clips, slides, and sound for my online courses so I can focus on my audience without distractions. He also helps with sound and registration for live events, as well as assisting me with any technology issues I have. There may have even been a few frantic late-night calls to him over the years when my printer decided to be difficult, and I needed handouts for a speaking engagement or workshop the next day! Curtis is the best. Finally, I have the most magnificent photographer who helped me create the cover of this book, who takes pictures of me for my website, social media posts, and promotional materials. Sarah Jane not only captures beautiful, timeless images with her camera, she also captures the energy and spirit of each person she photographs.

Whew! As you can see, it takes a village to run my life, and few things give me more joy than working with and benefitting from the gifts of all the people on this list. When I started my first business, it was just me and Jen, who was seventeen at the time. We worked side by side after school at the desk we squeezed into the tiny hot laundry room in my first seven-hundred-square-foot house. Over the years, I added another person and then another and another, and with each addition, my income and businesses grew. The process of finding great people and letting them help me is an area of genius that seems so easy to me, I don't even realize I do it! However, I've learned over the years that not everyone can spot talent as easily as I can, not everyone is as *open* to accepting help as I am, and not everyone can so quickly see how another person's natural genius can support their goals or family.

Now It's *Your* Turn

In his book *Atomic Habits*, James Clear offers a few questions that may help you identify *your* natural genius. One of my favorites is this one: "What feels like fun to me, but work to others?"

This question makes me think of my friend Mary, whom I met twenty years ago when we were both first-year high school teachers. She was an absolute joy to work with, and she made subjects like chemistry and biology both fun and approachable for her students. Mary is still teaching high school science, and I recently saw this posted on her Facebook wall: "I had a student tell me that my classroom was like walking into a hug. #room44adventures #bestcompliment #teachingismyjam."

How great is that? I'm not sure, but I'm guessing that to *most* people, engaging fourteen-to-eighteen-year-old human beings in learning about science is *not* fun, but to Mary it is a blast and a role that maximizes her unique gifts!

Here are a few more questions that Clear asks in his book that I love for their capacity to help find your genius:

- "What makes me lose track of time?"
- "Where do I get greater returns than the average person?"
- "What comes naturally to me?"

I also love this question Gay Hendricks poses about identifying your natural genius in his book *The Big Leap*, "In my work, what produces the highest ratio of abundance and satisfaction to amount of time spent? (Even if I do only ten seconds or a few minutes of it, an idea or a deeper connection may spring forth that leads to huge value.)"

When you figure out what this thing is that you do that feels easy to you and not so much to everyone around you, I want you to recognize its value. Because our areas of genius feel so easy to us, we tend to not recognize what they are worth. On a podcast with Brené Brown, Priya Parker shared a story about not only recognizing your natural genius but making sure you are adequately paid for what it is worth. She said that she was working with a business coach in a group of female entrepreneurs, and the coach was walking around the room challenging the members of the group on their pricing for their goods and services.

Parker said, "She looked at our prices and she kept on saying, 'Why is that number so low?' And different people, myself included, would say, 'I can do that in my sleep,' or 'That's really easy for me,' and [the coach] said, 'If that's really easy for you, that is your gift, and you should be charging the most for that.'"

Find the thing that feels easy to you and astonishes everyone else. Pursue it, use it, *max it out* because it is yours to nurture and to steward. Do that thing that feels easy to you and astonishes everyone else. Do as much of it as you possibly can! You will be fulfilled and energized, and the world will benefit from it too. And while you are doing it, recognize its value and don't you dare undercharge for it!

CHAPTER 2 EXERCISE
SEE YOUR OWN GENIUS

Pull out your journal and spend some time pondering your areas of unique genius. Seeing it in black and white can bring a lot of clarity.

- What are the things I do on a daily basis that feel so easy to me but that astonish everyone else?

- What am I doing when hours pass but I barely notice because I'm so engrossed in the experience?

- Am I currently receiving any form of financial compensation for the use of these unique gifts?

- Am I undervaluing myself in these areas or not being adequately compensated because using my gifts feels so easy to me?

- What would be the tiniest step I could take toward being paid to use these gifts or being compensated more than I currently am?

3

Stop Giving So Much

RIGHT AFTER Simone Biles decided to withdraw from the 2020 Olympic games in Tokyo because of concerns about her mental and emotional health, I was scrolling through Facebook and came upon a compelling post written by an eighth-grade English teacher from Utah named Byron Heath. The post had gone viral—shared over 500,000 times—and had been discussed on television as well. In his post, Heath describes proudly sitting down with his two young daughters to get them ready for the Olympics by showing them a video of one of his favorite Olympic memories: the vault pass gymnast Kerri Strug did on one leg in 1996.

In case you aren't familiar with the story, the US gymnastics team had a significant lead over the Russians heading into the final rotation of events; however, if the team's performance on the vault was poor, it would open the door for the Russians to potentially take the medal. Four American gymnasts vaulted before Strug, all struggling to land without any extra steps and hops that result in deductions from their scores. Then the exceptionally talented Dominique Moceanu unexpectedly fell not once but twice, earning a very low final score. Kerri Strug's vault was the final chance for the

American team to secure a definite victory over the Russians. On her first attempt, Strug landed awkwardly, fell, and violently twisted her ankle.

I vividly remember sitting on the edge of the couch in my basement watching the dramatic scene that unfolded next. Obviously in significant pain, Strug limped slowly back to the starting line while looking over at Béla Károlyi, the famous US team gymnastics coach. He looked into her terrified eyes and said, "We got to go one more time. Shake it out." Strug wiped her tears, turned to face the vault, took a deep breath, and ran the length of the mat as if for a few seconds the injury had never happened. She catapulted herself off the springboard on her hands and into the air, executed her numerous twists and turns and flips and then she stuck the landing perfectly, raising her arms proudly, then collapsing in pain moments later. The entire country, including me, stood from our couches to cheer and celebrate this brave victory over the Russians.

According to his story on Facebook, almost twenty-five years after this historic victory, Heath's young girls did not respond as he originally had when they watched the scene unfold. They didn't applaud Strug's bravery as he expected they might; rather, they expressed deep concern, asking why she jumped again if she was so obviously hurt.

Heath continues, "I made some inane reply about the heart of a champion or Olympic spirit, but in the back of my mind, a thought was festering: 'She shouldn't have jumped again.'"

Horrified, I realized after reading this young father's post, that I, too, had always celebrated Strug's injured vault as one of the greatest moments in US Olympic history. I watched every interview she did in the weeks following the Olympics, talked about it with friends and family, and raised Strug up as an American hero.

If you get the chance, I'd encourage you to find a video of the vault and watch it again. Should we have celebrated Kerri Strug's accomplishment? Or was what happened actually deeply damaging and misguided? Did anyone consider the physical and emotional health of a young girl, or were we just swept up in our insatiable national desire to win? Did it so fit our overarching narrative that women should sacrifice themselves for the good of others that we didn't even notice or question our celebration of her pain?

The part of the story no one ever talks about, and that fewer people even know is that the injury sustained in that vault forced Strug's retirement from gymnastics at the young age of eighteen. Heath continues in his post:

[Kerri Strug and Dominique Moceanu] were top gymnasts literally pushed to the breaking point, and then put out to pasture. Coach Karolyi and Larry Nassar (the serial sexual abuser) continued their long careers, while the athletes were treated as a disposable resource.

Today Simone Biles—the greatest gymnast of all time— chose to step back from the competition, citing concerns for mental and physical health. I've already seen comments and posts about how Biles "failed her country," "quit on us," or "can't be the greatest if she can't handle the pressure."

The subtext here is: "Our gold medal is more important than your well-being."

Let that sink in for a moment.

Is any athletic accomplishment, even on a global scale, more important than a human being's health and well-being? Simone Biles didn't feel she could safely perform her routine without endangering herself. So, with one very public, brave, and controversial choice, Biles said to *all* of us, *My physical and emotional health are more important than any medal.*

My value is not rooted in my ability to perform a routine with my body for your enjoyment and feeling of victory.

As a former collegiate athlete and recovering overachiever, I won't say her decision didn't feel a touch uncomfortable. After all, Biles had trained with such incredible focus and intensity for so many years in preparation for this one moment, and she also wasn't just any gymnast, but the greatest female gymnast of all time. Sponsors, television networks, teammates, and an entire nation were counting on her to be a highlight of the Olympics, on the biggest stage available to gymnasts, at a nationally televised event that happens only every four years. At her age, she might not have another opportunity of this magnitude. This was it. This was everything she had been training for her entire life!

And what did she do? She walked away. (I think it's important to note here that three years later, Biles is back and competing at the highest levels again *because* she had the courage to walk away when she did.)

The more I wrestled with my own response to her decision, the more I realized that the reason it was so difficult to digest is because it challenged every single woman, including me, to consider this: if Simone Biles could say no, under that kind of pressure and in that kind of a worldwide spotlight, then don't we all have permission to do the same under virtually *any* circumstance? With one decision, Biles taught us all that whether in the board room, within familial relationships, or on the balance beam, women should not be asked to destroy themselves to meet the needs of everyone else.

Unlike Biles, most women give and give without even considering their own well-being. We overwork our way to the top of the corporate food chain, sacrifice our physical well-being because we are so intent on selling more gadgets than any of our peers or earning the next promotion or pay raise, and we don't even consider our own emotional health when we say yes to one more family obligation or volunteer role. The truth is, you *can* increase your influence, impact, and income without destroying yourself in the process. But first, you have to unearth some deeply rooted harmful stories about what healthy giving looks like, and you've got to learn to say no.

The Giving Tree Is Not an Exemplary Model of Giving

Growing up, one of my favorite books that my mom read to me before bed was *The Giving Tree* by Shel Silverstein. I absolutely *love* the writing of Shel Silverstein. His collection of poetry titled *Where the Sidewalk Ends* was one of my childhood anthems. In my grade school years, I could recite the majority of "Sarah Cynthia Silvia Stout Would Not Take the Garbage Out" by heart, and I often laughed out loud at his clever poems, like "Crocodile's Toothache" in which an arrogant dentist is eaten by a crocodile while attempting to clean its many teeth.

However, in a children's literature course I took while working on my master's degree, I read *The Giving Tree* with fresh eyes. In case you aren't familiar, the story is about a female tree's sacrifice for the love of a boy. At first, the boy and the tree are friends, and they enjoy each other's company every day. The boy would pick up the tree's leaves and make them into a crown and pretend he was "king of the forest."

When the boy grows up, he wants a house, a family, and to see the world. So, the tree gives the boy her apples to sell, her branches to build a house, and her trunk to make a boat. Over and over, after some sacrifice on the part of the tree, the book tells us, "And then the boy was happy."

The truth is, you *can* increase your influence, impact, and income without destroying yourself in the process.

By the end of their relationship, the tree is nothing but a stump, and the boy is a tired old man needing a quiet place to rest. He sits down on the stump and the book says anew, "And the tree was happy."

As I dug into my analysis, questions about the meaning behind this bestselling book flooded my mind. Particularly for women, is the moral of the story healthy? And how pervasive is this message that we so easily embrace it as "good"? Is destroying yourself for another person something that should be celebrated? I vividly remember sitting alone at the desk in my apartment after rereading the story, wanting to indignantly argue with Silverstein: "Really? The tree was happy? The tree is not even a tree anymore. How could she be happy? She gave herself away completely! I don't know any people who give themselves away to this degree who are truly happy. I'm not buying it."

Now let's be clear. I have no idea what Silverstein's true intention was in writing the story, and I've read many different interpretations of the book. Some believe the tree represents the earth and the way we have treated the earth, which then makes the message a little more palatable, but most people see the book as a representation of a mom parenting her son or a woman caring for her male spouse. In my humble opinion, if this story represents the ideal experience of motherhood or of being a wife, I think the message stinks. Even more, if the story represents the overall expected role of women in our world, I am vehemently opposed.

Happiness in parenting or in life and particularly in our work does not come from giving myself away until all I am is a *stump* upon which someone can sit! No thank you! Yet, so many of the widely accepted and celebrated cultural messages that we receive, especially as women, are about giving ourselves away, putting others' needs before our own, making sure everyone around us is happy before we take care of ourselves. But at what cost? Is this really healthy?

I would like to offer some revised renditions of the tale. Perhaps when the boy is a grown man, returning to the tree, he says, "I am too busy to climb trees. I want a house to keep me warm. I want a wife and I want children, and so I need a house. Can you give me a house?" In response, the tree could say something like, "I'm so sorry. If I cut off my branches and give them to you so you can build a house, then I will have no leaves and no fruit for all of the other people who depend on me to provide for them. I'm grateful for you and our relationship, but I cannot give you a house."

Or perhaps even more bravely, the tree could follow the example of Simone Biles and simply say, "No, I cannot. If I give you my branches, I would be seriously and irreparably injured. But you can come back in a few years when I am rested and see what I can do for you then." Maybe the tree could simply say no without needing to explain herself at all. The story could still end with the words "And the tree was happy." And this time, the happiness would flow from *wholeness*, not from the destruction of self.

Playwright Topher Payne offers a wonderful alternate ending to the book in his Topher Fixed It series for young people. He writes,

And as each generation played in her strong old branches, the tree often thought back to the fateful day when the boy had asked her for a house. In truth, she would have gladly given him her branches to build one. She would have given him her trunk to build a boat. She loved him that much. But then she would have had nothing left. Not for herself, nor anyone else. And there never would have been a home for the red squirrels. There'd have been no hide and seek with the boy's grandchildren. No bakery with the best apple pies anyone ever tasted! Setting healthy boundaries is a very important part of giving. It assures you'll always have something left to give. And so the tree was happy. Everyone was. The End.

After all, it isn't healthy or inspiring for women to imagine that our highest goal in life is to wind up as a stump, someone that those we love destroyed in their self-serving attempts to get what they want. We can give of our time, talent, and treasure from the *overflow* and not sacrifice ourselves in the process. What if we volunteer in places that are important to us for a number of hours that don't cause us to feel resentful and taken advantage of? What if we give a percentage of our financial resources, with intention and generosity, while still keeping enough to comfortably take care of our own needs? What if we agree to watch our grandchildren when it feels like we are giving a gift, not every time we are asked? What if we only served on one board, leaving most of our evenings free for our families, instead of serving on four or five? I want to challenge all of us to redefine giving and to think of giving the fruit of our branches—that can be constantly replenished—while we maintain strong branches and a healthy trunk.

The better we get at taking care of us, the more everyone wins. We don't have to destroy ourselves to get what we want. Actually, for most of us, the key to getting to the next level of income, influence, and impact is to slow down and take care of ourselves at a higher level than we ever have before. We must reject the insipient, sneaky thought habit that tells us that progress comes only from an unhealthy level of self-sacrifice.

The Parable of the Golden Goose

During one particularly exhausting season of growing my business, I worked with a coach named Dr. Nathan Baxter. Dr. Baxter often challenged me with a parable he referred to as "The Golden Goose." I return to this parable often when I'm tempted to push through and neglect my own needs, especially when work or my home life is very demanding. I'd love to challenge you with my expanded, somewhat embellished version of it too.

Imagine for a moment that you own a goose who lays golden eggs. Every day, you gather the eggs, and these golden treasures provide for all of your family's needs. Because there are so many and because they are so valuable, the eggs have created a great deal of wealth that provides for your family's *wants* as well.

Consider for a moment how you would care for your very valuable, rare goose who lays these golden eggs. Would you make sure the goose had the best nutrition that money could buy? Would you allow it to get incredibly hungry and then stuff it full of food when you had a quick minute, or would you feed it at regular intervals throughout the day?

Would you be sure the goose maintained a healthy body that was optimal in strength and capacity for laying golden eggs? Would you make sure that your goose got out of its pen and exercised regularly so it was strong and would live a long, healthy life?

What would the living conditions be like for your goose? Would you fill its pen with junk that it didn't really need but that you mindlessly bought on Amazon while lying on the couch watching television at night? Or would you clear the clutter and make sure the goose's living space was fresh, well lit, and cleaned on a regular basis?

What if there was a mean, abusive goose in the pen with your goose, what would you do then? Would you eliminate that abusive goose from its environment no matter how disruptive the removal was or how long or costly the battle was to protect your goose?

Would you make sure the goose was happy and had great friends? And that it got to see those friends on a regular basis to laugh and talk and connect?

What if the goose was sick or had a bad foot and it was limping or what if it had a sore under its feathers or a spot on one of its webbed feet? Would you take it to the doctor right away?

If the goose got depressed or very anxious, would you call a goose mental health care professional *immediately* to set up an appointment?

If the goose needed any kind of medicine or vitamins, would you make sure it took them on a daily basis?

And how about sleep? Would you let the goose stay up all night playing on its electronic devices, or would you make sure it got a full night's sleep?

Am I correct in assuming that you would do everything you could to make sure that goose who laid the golden eggs that provided for your family's wants and needs was healthy, happy, and comfortable?

I think it's clear where I'm going with all of this. And I hope at least one question I asked made you a *little* uncomfortable, because this is important for you to internalize: You are the golden goose! You are the one who lays the golden eggs! You are the one who provides for your family! You are rare and valuable, and you have the ability to create a great deal of wealth and abundance!

So why don't you treat yourself like a goose who lays golden eggs and has great value instead of a pauper? You put everyone else's needs before your own, and you neglect your body and your mental and emotional health, and then the craziest part of all, you wonder why your eggs are small or lumpy or, even worse, brown and not golden! You ignore lingering health issues instead of attacking them. You neglect your body but expect it to perform at peak levels of energy for long periods of time. You don't regularly fill your cup with healthy friendships and relationships. You feel guilty paying money to take care of yourself, and then you wonder why you aren't producing any more golden eggs!

Often, after sharing this parable with my clients, they act on things they have been procrastinating on for a while. One client went to the dentist for the first time in five years; another hired a professional organizer to help her revamp her cluttered, overwhelming office space; and yet another called to schedule an appointment with a highly recommended therapist whose number she had saved in her phone for years. We don't need to address all of the areas of self-care at once, but taking small steps in these ways feels incredibly empowering. It's a tangible way to say to the world, "I am worth taking care of. I deserve to be treated with love and respect. I don't have to destroy myself in the service of others."

You can't lead with confidence and energy if you're sick or injured. You aren't able to make the best decisions when you're overtired or depressed. You don't respond with patience or empathy when you are emotionally drained and overwhelmed. And the people around you need you at your best. If you are a leader, often the greatest gift you can give others is taking care of yourself.

The better we get at taking care of us, the more everyone wins.

CHAPTER 3 EXERCISE
GOLDEN GOOSE SELF-ASSESSMENT

Pull out your journal and answer the questions in each of the following categories.

Living and working conditions

- What is my emotional response to my living conditions? Do they make me feel peaceful, calm, and safe?

- Is there any area of my living space that needs to be decluttered? (Take time right now to schedule this activity on your calendar. If there are lots of areas, pick the worst one and schedule a time to work on just that one!)

- What physical items are draining my financial resources and need to be thrown away, donated, or sold?

- How do I feel when I walk into my workspace? Is that space—whether it be inside or outside the home—conducive to me doing my best work?

- If working from home, do I need to create a space that is separate from my living space so I know when I am "at work" and when I am "at home"?

Physical health

- Am I fueling my body with food and drink that provide my body with the best energy and allowing it to reach peak—or even satisfactory—performance?

- If I keep eating and drinking the way I am right now, what will happen to my body in five years? Ten years? Fifteen years? Twenty years?

- If I don't like the results of my choices in twenty years, what accountability or help do I need to seek out in this area in order to be able to write down a different answer?

- What doctor, specialist, dentist, or naturalist do I need to contact to take care of myself or things I've been ignoring? Is there any medication I should be taking that I am neglecting to take? Do I need to reassess my health insurance in order to receive the care I need but have neglected to address?

- How are my sleep patterns? Am I getting enough rest to perform at my best and to be fully present in my life?

- Are there any habits—alcohol, smoking, or drugs—that are hindering my quality of life or that don't allow me to be my best? Am I using any substances to escape from stress or to cope with pain in my life? Do I need to seek help to eliminate them from my life?

Mental health

- If I have felt anxious, sad, or depressed, how long have these feelings persisted? Would my spouse or children or those closest to me say my mental health is affecting my relationship with them?

- Is there trauma in my past that I've never dealt with that continues to affect my life every day? Do I need to enlist the help of a professional to help me safely address this unhealed pain?

4

You Don't Have to Work More

W HEN I was a brand-new leader, with only a small number of people on my team, I often felt consumed by a deep responsibility to make sure *every* person I led was happy and that they *all* were successful. I felt like I needed to answer every text, every email, every phone call immediately because they needed me if they all were going to succeed. Evenings weren't really time away from work but an extension of it. Even vacations were full of "urgent" calls and messages that needed my attention. Because my business was so new and small, I felt like this was necessary, especially if I was going to survive financially for those lean first years of entrepreneurship. However, this self-imposed expectation created a very fragile dynamic in my organization that looked like a bicycle tire with long thin spokes. I was at the center of the wheel, and all the spokes led to me.

In the middle of that stressful and exhausting season of almost nonstop availability, a wise mentor overheard me on the phone handling a sticky customer situation that really wasn't my responsibility. I didn't trust the person on my team whose job it was to handle these situations as well as I thought I could. After I hung up from the call, this mentor asked me a life-changing question: "Can you do for one hundred people what you just did for that one?"

At first, I felt defensive. What was wrong with helping someone navigate a difficult conversation? After all, I had plenty of time in my day for these conversations because my business was still small. I needed every possible customer if we were going to survive. Pretty quickly, though, my mind started thinking through a few of the other things I had done that week for the people I led. I started filtering each situation through the question I'd just been asked.

Could I completely interrupt the workflow of my day to call corporate headquarters to find out whether our products have gluten in them for one hundred salespeople under my leadership like I just did for that one? Could I stop what I was doing to find the link to the product shade conversion chart for one hundred people like I just did for that one? Could I disrupt my work to find a phone number for one hundred team members when it was easily accessible on the company website?

My stomach sank with the realization that my constant availability was very likely the reason that my organization wasn't growing. Yes, my constant availability was helping those I led immediately, but it was not creating independent problem-solvers who could figure out issues on their own.

If that wasn't enough, this wise person who asked me this life-altering question then quietly said, "If the answer is no, you can't do for one hundred people what you just did for that one, and you continue to do those things, then you will never lead one hundred people." It was a turning point in my leadership. I started to run everything I did through this filter question.

Can I do _____ (which I'm doing for this one person)
for one hundred people?

I started being slow to answer urgent requests for information, and to my surprise, my team started to find the answers on their own. I started to refer their questions to other available resources. I was their leader, but I did not have to be the only source of answers and solutions. Slowly but surely, the less I did for people, the more my business grew.

When I got to the place where I was leading one hundred people, I changed the filter to two hundred. A paradoxical truth about leadership is that the more people you lead, the less you can do for them, particularly things that they can do themselves.

To clarify this concept even further, another dear friend taught me during this season that my role as a leader was not to be a vending machine. A *vending machine*? Yes, that contraption to which people come, insert a currency, and get rewarded with a snack or drink in return. The followers of vending machine leaders come to their leaders with their currency: a question. The leader then provides the instant reward of an answer. The follower learns that the leader is the source of all answers. Everyone depends on the leader to solve problems, answer questions, and to move forward in their own growth and journeys. That's not healthy or realistic for a leader of a larger organization.

One of the people I lead once said to me, "I was going to call you and ask you a question, but then I knew you would say, 'What would *you* do?' So I asked myself that, and I went and did it! It was *awesome!*" I laughed out loud when I hung up the phone with her and celebrated how far I had come. By changing how I thought of my role as a leader and showing up differently, I was proving every day that you really could increase your influence, impact, and income without increasing the number of hours you work. What a relief!

How to Turn Off the Vending Machine

If you have just realized that you are a vending machine leader, here are a few suggestions to help you turn it off. First, start connecting the people you lead with other people on your team or in your network who are great at answering those questions, the experts on any particular subject. I often say something like, "You know who would know more than I do about that? Stacy! She's a technology whiz!" When you connect them with more people who can help them find answers, they start developing their own network of resources and start tapping into that network before coming to you.

Next, delay your responses. Don't answer the email, text, or call immediately. If you always answer right away, they learn that you are available for instant responses, which increases the likelihood they'll come to you before exploring any other option. Do you stop everything you're doing every time you hear a ping on your computer or phone? What if you only checked email two or three times a day, and then when you did, what if you gave it a full forty-five minutes of attention? I dare you to wait twenty-four to forty-eight hours before you respond to a request, even when you know it could cause that person to struggle a bit. In my experience, the person asking the "urgent" question will go find the answer if you aren't always at their beck and call.

I'd also challenge you to examine the motives behind your availability. Do you need to be needed? (Warning: if this is how you are at work, work's probably not the only place this pattern shows up.) Are you worried that you'll look less strong, more vulnerable, or less useful if you don't solve every problem? If you aren't available instantly to everyone, will you then have to address larger projects that you are putting off because they feel daunting or scary? Do the constant interruptions relieve you from having to do more challenging or vulnerable work? Busy is a very safe place to hide in plain sight.

Also keep in mind that shutting down the vending machine will not initially be a popular decision. Just as toddlers sometimes kick and scream when you institute new rules, adults will protest and often in strong, visible ways. Remember, you created the mess so you can *un*-create it as well; just be warned, there *will be* pushback to the changes you make. That's okay. It means you're growing and changing. You may even need to be direct with some individuals and say something like, "I am creating some new boundaries on my availability to make room for growth, so I may not be as available to you immediately as I have been in the past. I'll get back to you, but it won't always be as quickly. I'm trusting you to find some solutions and answers on your own. You are ready, and I know you can do it."

The bottom line is that our role as a leader is to ask questions, to listen, to occasionally provide tools, to believe in people, and to empower people. Our job is not to solve their problems and answer every question they have. It's to teach them how to solve and answer them on their own.

As I grew in my confidence as a leader, I would often challenge myself with this question in every interaction: *Am I just answering the question, or am I coaching people to answer their own questions?* As this became my primary question, I also realized that the size of my business was starting to grow way beyond me, and I was working fewer hours than I ever had before. It was obvious that by focusing on developing independent, strong people, the business and my income and impact could continue to grow without my having to work more hours.

My constant availability was very likely impeding our organization's growth.

Work Less and Play More

I also learned in this season that the *best* thing I could do for the growth of my business and for those I lead was to rest and to have more fun when I wasn't working. When I worked all the time, or even when I was *thinking* about work all the time, everyone got a tired, emotionally drained version of me. I wasn't showing up at my best for the people I worked with or for my family at home. At about the same time, a trusted friend recommended the book *The Now Habit* by Neil Fiore, and I was introduced to the concept of "scheduled guilt-free play."

Fiore writes, "A firm commitment to guilt-free play will recharge your batteries, creating renewed motivation, creativity, and energy for all the other areas of your life. Knowing that work will not deprive you of enjoying the good things of life, you can more easily tackle a large task without the fear of having it rule your life. Knowing that work on a large task will be interrupted by commitments to friends, to exercise, and to free time, you can approach the task with less fear of being overwhelmed."

Our adult brains want to separate work and play, and they tend to categorize play as frivolous and unnecessary. However, the investment of significant amounts of time and money in fun, unstructured play is a characteristic of the most influential change agents in our world. Contrary to the messaging of most American work environments, we are *much* more likely to work productively when we can anticipate experiences we genuinely enjoy on a regular basis rather than only having our efforts lead to isolation, anxiety, or more work.

When I first started working with a client I will call Erica in the spring a few years ago, she had recently left a corporate setting and started her own business. She was working about seventy hours a week, often coming home at seven or eight at night and collapsing from exhaustion only to start all over again the next day. Her business was solid but not growing as quickly as she wanted, and the weight of responsibility and pressure on her shoulders felt crippling. She hired me because she wanted me to help grow her income and the size of her client base so she could finally stop working so much and enjoy the perks of entrepreneurship. You can imagine her surprise when my first challenge to her was to open her datebook and block out all of her time off for the summer months. I wanted her to schedule her vacations, her days off, and even decide what her summer hours would be. I also asked her to do an audit of her calendar to see how much guilt-free play was currently scheduled for these months or to see if there was any at all.

She returned to our next session with three important things to tell me. The first was that she had completed her first homework assignment from me, and she had actually blocked off every Friday between Memorial Day and Labor Day in her calendar along with a week-long vacation with her husband in July. The second was that the self-audit of her calendar showed she had *nothing* fun actually scheduled for the next few months, only work commitments. This realization felt draining and overwhelming, and it also carried with it a bit of guilt and resignation. She wanted to have *more* time with her family and friends when she became an entrepreneur, not less, but this felt impossible if she also wanted to achieve her financial goals. Finally, she said, "I'm going to be very direct here. I'm terrified. I hired you to help me increase the size of my business and you are telling me I need to work *less* than I do right now? I don't see how this is ever going to work."

I thanked Erica for her honesty and frankness, and then I explained that the first step in becoming more productive for most overachievers is to actually schedule their guilt-free recreational time. Guilt-free playtime can be dinner with a dear friend, time to read a juicy romance novel, participating in a sport or activity you enjoy like biking or golf, a long walk with a partner or spouse, or anything that leaves you feeling rejuvenated and energized. Having these activities on your calendar gives you the feeling that your life is full of things you love; it isn't just a never-ending stream of work obligations that keep you from the activities and people you love most.

I assured Erica that her fears were normal and to be expected, and I asked her to trust me. Her next assignment was to schedule the fun things she loves to do most for the next few months, particularly those involving the people who are most important to her. For someone like Erica, commitments to work fewer hours, to leave work on time or earlier, are typically short-lived and easily broken. The pull of working "just another fifteen minutes" quickly stretches into an hour and the cycle of overworking continues indefinitely. However, what if Erica has a monthly dinner with her best girlfriends at her favorite restaurant in the calendar at six that night? Or a cookout with some of her cousins scheduled for Thursday at five thirty? Or a weekend trip with her husband to their cabin in Michigan planned, and they are leaving at four o'clock on Friday? I know Erica, and if these commitments are in her calendar, she will move mountains to get her work done on time so she can leave the office!

In *The Now Habit*, Fiore argues that the most important step in getting more done is to *first* schedule time off for guilt-free play. Without even trying consciously, scheduled playtime causes you to become more productive. When you have something to look forward to at the end of your work, you tend to get more done and to get it done more efficiently. In addition, when you feel great about the work you've done because you've been more focused, you can head out of the office to fully enjoy the rest of your life. Finally, Fiore contends that guilt-free play stimulates new ideas and more creative thinking, which leads to a better overall quality of work. You start to see solutions instead of obstacles. Your subconscious mind gets to play while you play, coming up with fresh perspectives and connections. Fiore explains, "This can happen when you are relaxed because while your conscious mind is focused somewhere else for two hours of guilt-free play, your creative, subconscious mind can provide clear, almost effortless solutions."

I want you to remember the most important thing in this cycle. Where does it all begin? It doesn't begin with working longer hours or by sacrificing your quality of life for your work. Everything starts with scheduling the things you most love to do away from your work! You can use this principle throughout your workday by building in breaks and rewards after sessions of intense work. If your brain knows that after you finish working on payroll for thirty minutes, you get to take a fruit and coffee break, or that you get to scroll through Facebook and see what everyone is up to for just ten minutes, you will attack your work with more zest and energy! When you build enjoyment and play into your schedule in small doses, your days will feel lighter and the tasks that you dislike or tend to procrastinate on won't feel so heavy.

The truth is that people who accomplish the most are deeply committed to their leisure time. Their health and recreation are high priorities. They swim, run, or exercise regularly. They have dinner with friends. They spend quality time with family. They don't see work as depriving them of anything, but they work intensely, and they play intensely. Mostly, they are *living now*, not only after all of their work is completed!

For example, I know at the end of this very jam-packed day, full of client appointments, meetings, and writing, I get to go play pickleball with a group of friends. Thinking ahead to a game I love enables me to focus on the task in front of me more fully. In addition, on Saturday, we leave for a fun vacation to Cancun. I can imagine the warmth of the sun on my skin and the feeling of my toes in the sand even as I type. Because I have these things to look forward to, I am using the time I have wisely to complete my most important tasks.

If you need more proof that this works, consider when you get more done—the week before vacation or the week after? If you're like me, it's always the week before, when I know a fun reward is coming! When are you more energized about your work? Before or after a scheduled break? I always work with a higher level of focus and energy before an upcoming trip.

A reminder that this also works on a smaller scale. I can fill my cup by scheduling smaller chunks of guilt-free play every day after I finish work tasks. Some of my favorites are so simple: reading funny memes on social media late in the afternoon; listening to one of my favorite podcasts; stopping in for a late afternoon shaved ice at my local candy shop; visiting with Ryan's grandparents who live at a nearby assisted living facility; making a quick stop at my favorite shop to buy a shirt I've been eyeing; taking a short walk, a bike ride, a yoga class; grabbing coffee with a friend; watching an episode of *Madam Secretary* or *Ted Lasso*; or reading a fun book. Even driving in my car alone singing my favorite songs at the top of my lungs refills my cup!

I also have learned that I require at least one "adventure" a month to keep my motivation high and to feel inspired and stay focused. In the past few years, our family has gone ziplining in the Rocky Mountains; driven ATVs in the mountains in Utah; survived some intense, white-knuckled white water rafting at Yosemite Park; and we enjoyed a guided three-hour Segway tour through the Garden of the Gods. I traveled to New York City in November with two girlfriends to see three shows in one weekend on Broadway, and we take regular weekend trips to watch our daughter play college volleyball. These adventures give me energy and passion for what I do; they are a vital part of my success. It took me years to stop feeling like I *should* be working instead of playing, but I have shifted and now see them as priceless investments *in* my work. Adventures help me feel like the work I do is creating a life I love, which makes me grateful, not resentful.

And Erica? I had a call with her last week. She had just returned from a week-long trip to an island in the Caribbean, she already has her Fridays blocked off from Memorial Day to Labor Day for this coming summer, and without even trying, she now leaves the office no later than five o'clock each day. In addition, her business is thriving, and she is earning three times more than she did when we started working together, all while working fewer hours than ever before. This didn't happen overnight, but with each brave step away from old patterns of overworking, her income grew, and she attracted clients who were more enjoyable to work with and who generated more profit. Occasionally, old thought habits that tell her she should be working more still creep in—she needs accountability to make sure she has enough fun in her schedule—but she can catch these thoughts so much more quickly now and choose a different perspective. After all, her business is not her entire life; it's a vehicle through which she is creating the life of her dreams!

We Are Designed to Live in Rhythms

Scheduling free time and play into our lives also makes sense given that we live in rhythms. Our physical world has seasons, and seasons are rhythms. Sometimes it's freezing cold. Sometimes it's steaming hot. Sometimes it's mild and in the middle. Our lives have rhythms. The tyrannical tempo of toddlerhood slows to the moderate dance of adulthood and then on to the wandering waltz of old age. Our weeks have rhythms. There is a sputtering start, a crescendo in the middle, and a sweet, anticipated end. Our days have rhythms. There are mornings, afternoons, and then evenings—and then we sleep. And of course, art that speaks to us deeply has rhythms. For example, music. Songs slow and speed up, they are soft and then they are loud, taking us on a journey through their rises and falls. We connect with rhythms because we are created to live in them. Expecting that every element of every day of your life will be structured is unrealistic, unhealthy, and ignores our need for rhythms. We can focus intently on our work, but then we need rest. Simply put, there is no way to sustain structure and focus over the long haul if you do not have a break from it.

When I started my coaching business, I put into place some structures to protect myself from my workaholic tendencies and to honor the rhythms of my internal energy. Overachievers like me often set goals without considering their personal work-life capacity. My number one goal in this business is to work my business like a teacher and get paid like a ceo. This means I work traditional school hours: Monday through Friday between the hours of eight and three, having holidays, evenings, and weekends off, with a much lighter workload in the summer, all while getting paid the wages of a ceo. I've incorporated my own best daily, weekly, monthly, and annual rhythms into the design of my schedule. While this schedule full of breaks and rest may sound blissful and easy, you better believe my boundaries protecting it get tested on a regular basis.

For example, I recently had a conversation with a female executive who was a perfect prospective client for the work I do. At the end of our hour together, I was telling her I typically meet with clients every other week for an hour spread out over six to seven months. She said, "That's great. I can meet any day of the week at five thirty or six in the evening." When I asked if she was available during the day, she said, "Oh, shoot. I'm not. I have to be available for my colleagues, and there are constant interruptions."

I took a deep breath to slow myself down. *Everything* in me wanted to make an exception. She is what I lovingly call "my people." She is the exact person I created this company to serve. And I *knew* I could help her. Couldn't I just make one tiny exception this time? I asked her if I could get back to her the following day after I thought it over (a little trick I've learned to protect me from my own negative thought habits and to give myself a fighting chance against deeply ingrained habits of overworking).

When I called her back the following day, I simply said, "I would love nothing more than to work with you. However, if I violate my own boundaries and say yes, I would not be able to lead you through this work with any kind of integrity. If meeting during the day is impossible, I'm afraid this work won't serve either of us. I am so sorry."

There was a loss of opportunity to serve, a loss of income, and a loss of the chance to develop a meaningful relationship with a really cool leader. Boundaries that protect your rhythms are difficult. But I've found over the long run that my business grows with more consistency and joy when I

Am I just answering
the question,
or am I coaching
people to answer their
own questions?

don't resent it because I'm over-giving like in *The Giving Tree*. More fruit can grow when I don't hack off my branches in an attempt to help everyone who could benefit from my coaching.

The Six Most Important Things List

A practical tool that I use every single day to help me embrace the rhythms of work and rest as an entrepreneur is what I call a Six Most Important Things List. Let me start with a little history lesson on this tool, which has been a part of my daily life now for over twenty years. Its origins date back about a century.

In the early 1900s, Charles M. Schwab ran Bethlehem Steel. He was widely considered to be one of the wealthiest and most ambitious men in the world, and he was relentless in his pursuit of any strategies or tools that would improve his business and the productivity of his team. In 1918, Schwab reached out to a man named Ivy Lee, who was an expert in business efficiency.

James Clear imagines their conversation in his article titled "The Ivy Lee Method: The Daily Routine Experts Recommend for Peak Productivity":

"Give me fifteen minutes with each of your executives," Lee [said to Schwab in their first meeting].

"How much will it cost me?" Schwab asked.

"Nothing," Lee said. "Unless it works. After three months, you can send me a check for whatever you feel it's worth to you."

During their fifteen-minute conversations, Lee shared a simple process with each of the leaders in Schwab's organization. First, he asked the executives to make a written list at the end of each workday of only six important things they needed to do the following day. Then he told them to arrange those six things in order of importance, from top to bottom, prioritizing those things that were most impactful. Finally, when they came to work, they were to start with the first item on the list and then attack the second and so on only crossing items off the list that were finished. Any unfinished items were to be moved to the next day's list.

The simplicity of the process seemed too good to be true to a skeptical Schwab, but the team committed to the daily Six Most Important Things Lists and used them for a few months. Blown away by the results his team and the company achieved during the trial period, Schwab sent Lee a hefty check that would be worth nearly $500,000 today.

After more than two decades using this tool, I can personally attest to some of its benefits in my own life. In keeping with the spirit of the list, here are the six most important benefits I get from using it.

1   The list gives you a *finished* feeling

Let's face an unfiltered, hard-core truth together: leaders and entrepreneurs are never *fully* finished with their work. Even if you complete all the tasks on your list, most of the time, these completed tasks just create more to do. To sustain a pace that doesn't burn you out, leaders must *decide to be done* for the day. You will need small daily wins and a feeling of completion or else, eventually, you will burn out.

My client, whom I will call Tina, and her husband own and run a business together. They have about twenty employees and three very busy children, and they are very active in their community. When Tina first joined one of my coaching groups, she had a scattered energy surrounding her; she was flustered, frantic, and completely exhausted at all times. The first thing she implemented at the start of the engagement was using a Six Most Important Things List.

By the end of our four months together, she looked and sounded like a different person. It was as if she had her feet under her again. She said, "It felt like my brain would never stop spinning. I was worrying about home and the kids at work, and then at home I was doing all kinds of work. The work I did in this group has helped me to be present where I am, and the Six Most Important Things List is one of the most important tools I use to make sure that happens. My list tells me when I can shut the door to my office and head home, feeling accomplished and finished."

Personally, I love to have a little celebration at the end of the day when I've crossed important items off my list. Sometimes, it's just a private fist pump in my office that says to me, "Yes! I did what I said I was going to do today. *Everything* isn't done, but I made progress, and I can leave the office feeling great about what I did!"

2   **The list controls your pace**

Sprinting can be done in short bursts when needed to reach a milestone goal or to finish a big project, but it isn't a way of life. You've got to pace yourself if you're going to reach the end of the journey and look back on it with pride and joy instead of resentment and exhaustion. Businesses and careers will take as much from you as you allow them to take. The long-term success of what you are building depends on your being able to work at a sustainable pace for years, not just months or weeks at a time. The Six Most Important Things List acts like a governor on a golf cart: it slows you down when your pace gets too fast and protects your energy for the longer journey.

3 **The list allows you to maximize
the impact of small pockets of time**
I also think of the list like my anchor; it allows me to maximize the impact of small pockets of time. With my clients, I often refer to these as the "magic pockets" of the day. There are typically several points in my day when I have time before my next call or before I need to leave to get to an appointment or to pick up the kids from school. Each of those open twenty to forty-five minute intervals are critical moments of decision.

Start paying attention to these magic pockets in your own days. What is your habit during those small chunks of time? Do you tend to do *re*active things or *pro*active things? Do you open your inbox and start replying to the twenty new emails from current clients? Do you start to sift through texts on your phone—getting sidetracked into personal matters that really could wait until after your workday finishes? Do you open your online banking, then check your Facebook for new notifications, then your Instagram, and then head back to your email again? And by the time you've made these rounds and responded to everything, is that small chunk of time you had gone?

Capitalizing on the magic pockets means choosing proactive action steps over all this incessant noise. The only way I have a fighting chance against the temptation of all the busy work sitting on my desk is by looking at my Six Most Important Things List. Is there one item on the list that I can attack in the small chunk of time I have? Even if I can't finish it, can I *start* it?

Also, I don't have time to stop in those magic pockets of time to figure out *what* to do, but I *can* act on a list that is already created. One of the blessings of having three really busy kids, a husband, and a growing business is that there

Busy is a very
safe place to hide
in plain sight.

are very clear limitations on my time. When I have a snippet of time to work and everyone is at school, I have to work on the things that will make the greatest impact. It's amazing what can be accomplished when you have a clear Six Most Important Things List prepared in advance.

4   **The list provides accountability for the tasks you don't enjoy**

If you tend to be more of a "task" person, be sure there are "people" items on the list and put those at the top of the list to *start* with when you have your best energy. If you are a "people" person, start with the "task" items when you have your best energy and get them done first! I promise you'll still be engaged when it is time for the work that energizes you.

I love tasks. They are entirely in my control. This may sound contradictory given my work as a coach, but tasks don't talk back or make strange choices, and they are generally peaceful. People tend to be a little more erratic and draining to me, so I will avoid them if I'm tired or unmotivated or if I can accomplish a task instead. Because I recognize this tendency in myself, I try to make sure at least half of the items on my list involve interactions with people—outgoing contacts, follow-up conversations, and proactive networking efforts. Otherwise, I'll just have a very clean office and a very stagnant business. Some of you are the exact opposite. You probably already know who you are! Tasks can feel monotonous and boring, even stifling to you. If you love people, be sure your list has some tasks on it that you have been putting off or ignoring!

5   **You can be more present throughout the day**

A Six Most Important Things List allows you to plan the next day while being focused and present in the current day. I often make my list for the next day or even for a few days in the future as I'm working through my current day. When the completion of a task triggers something that needs to be done the following day or when a thought about something that needs to be done pops into my head unexpectedly, I simply flip to tomorrow's list in my notebook and add the task immediately. It keeps my brain from feeling like it is swirling in circles, and I can let go of that nagging feeling that there is so much to do and no planned time to do it.

6   **Using the list is a great opportunity for you to practice imperfect progress**

Guess what? You're not going to create a perfect Six Most Important Things List *every single day*. And you definitely aren't going to finish all six things every single day. This is a great opportunity to live out one of my favorite quotes one of my business coaches taught me: "Imperfect progress is better than perfect procrastination."

If you don't finish items on the list, simply move them to the next day. Sometimes, I just make the next day's list shorter, maybe only three items, and go back to what I didn't get done the day before. Expecting perfection with a tool like this is a losing battle. Imperfect progress is the goal.

I ALSO want to share with you my stupid-simple daily sheet where I write my Six Most Important Things List. Throughout the years, I've tried so many different task sheets and notebooks and calendars, and the one I come back to time and again is this one basic sheet I created myself. I print about thirty copies, hole punch them, and put them in a binder. I know there are more technology-savvy ways to do this, but there is something about putting a pen to paper that works better for me. Four days of Six Things Lists fit on one page, and I'll often use Fridays as a clean-up day to catch up on items I didn't get to earlier in the week. You can find this sheet on my website, AmyKemp.com.

IF YOU'VE never worked with a tool like this, I challenge you to try it out, even for just one week. Commit to making your list before the end of your workday or at least before you go to bed at night. And then *use it*, attack it in the magic pockets of your day. I know you'll be glad you did!

I'll wrap up with a reminder that your thought habits, which are designed with survival in mind, are probably going to scream at you at the top of their lungs when you embrace this new way of work and life. For years as I changed these habits, this is what mine sounded like, clamoring loudly in my head all day long. They would yell, "Danger! Danger! Danger! You cannot work *less* and *get* more! That doesn't make sense! You will fall behind. People will pass you by. You will fail! You need the money! Work more. Work more!"

These thought habits are a demanding, cruel boss. I learned to kindly and calmly acknowledge them and—often out loud to myself—say right back, "Thank you so much for your input. I hear you, and I acknowledge that your fear feels real, but it isn't. I am safe. I am showing up differently these days, full of belief that I can in fact create what I want with a new approach. I don't have to work longer hours in order to grow my influence, impact, or income. I just have to replace you with different thoughts. You've had your time to shine, but you are no longer needed here."

CHAPTER 4 EXERCISE
A CALENDAR AUDIT AND
A SIX MOST IMPORTANT THINGS LIST

Here are a few concrete action steps that can help you get more done—without working more—by employing what you learned in this chapter.

- Pull out your calendar and look at the next ninety days. How much *scheduled* guilt-free play is in there?

- I triple-dog (yep, I said it) dare you to increase what is there by just one step. If you have nothing scheduled currently, add one small fun activity to your calendar each month. If you have one thing scheduled each month, add one more. Maybe bump it up to one scheduled guilt-free playtime each week once you get good at scheduling at least two a month . . . You'll be amazed at how your productivity increases as the amount of guilt-free play in your schedule does!

- Do a test-run with a Six Most Important Things List. As I mentioned earlier, if you want to try using it, you can download the weekly sheet I use to make my lists on my website, AmyKemp .com.

5

Can I Get a
Little Woo-Woo?

OR ALMOST two years, I have been dealing with a nagging chronic pain in my left shoulder—all along my shoulder blade, up my neck, and down my arm. At the start of 2023, after it had gotten to the point where I was no longer able to sleep because the pain was so intense, I decided it was time to stop and solve the problem. I scheduled an appointment with my general practitioner and got a referral for physical therapy.

Prescription for three months of treatment in hand, off I went to see the physical therapist who had been highly recommended by a friend. After spending about an hour with me in conversation while contorting my body in about a hundred different ways, he concluded that the issue really wasn't in my shoulder, but in the way I was holding my neck and upper body. When I sit with my chin extended out in front of my body, looking at a computer or talking to people, the muscles along my shoulder blades have to hold the weight of my head. When those muscles eventually become fatigued, they spasm, and this was what was causing the pain.

At some point during our conversation, the physical therapist said to me, "Sometimes, people call me a healer, but I am not. All I do is to put your body into a position where it can heal itself. The body does the healing on its own if the conditions are right. Do you understand that?"

I said, "I understand perfectly. This is exactly the kind of internal work I do with my clients and their habits of thinking. When their thought habits are blocking their progress, they feel frustrated and discouraged. They feel pain of a different sort. As we identify those problematic habits of thinking and replace them with more beneficial thoughts, the flow of creativity through them and out into the world begins to flow again. All I'm doing is helping them clear the path."

This matter-of-fact interaction with my physical therapist inspired the idea for a brand-new webinar and even the name for that course and this chapter—"Can I Get a Little Woo-Woo?" It still makes me smile every time I read it or say it out loud because it can be said in the tone of an exuberant cheerleader, encouraging people to give you a little shout. woo-woo! Or it can be spoken with more of a teasing spiritual connotation, like we are stepping outside the boundaries of practical, rational thought to explore something a bit more... woo-woo.

Building a Foundation of Agreement

Let's start unpacking this woo-woo idea by building a foundation of core beliefs upon which we can agree. My clients are from all kinds of faith backgrounds and embrace all kinds of spiritual belief systems, but I've yet to have a client disagree with any of these five core statements:

1   There is a source of unlimited abundance and energy.

2   We are all created by this source.

3   We are all connected to this source.

4   If we open ourselves to it, the energy from this source flows through our unique gifts and into the world.

5   We feel most alive when we live in this flow.

If we can agree on these statements, I have a series of questions for you. What if our number one job in life is to simply allow powerful universal energy to flow through us and out into the world? What if everything we want and are trying to create depends on only one thing—how connected we are to the source from which all things come? What if we are all uniquely designed to create something or to serve the world in a specific way as universal energy flows through us? And if we are designed to be unique conduits, shouldn't we ruthlessly identify and eliminate any blockage that is inhibiting the flow of that energy?

Does all of that sound a little woo-woo? It certainly is! Let me say it to you again in this way because I find that the more it is repeated in new ways, the more it resonates: almost all people, who hold *all kinds* of spiritual beliefs, agree that we have access to a source of energy that is greater and more powerful than we are. This energy has been called Collective Conscious, the Holy Spirit, the Universe, Source Energy, God, Allah, and many other names. There are so many words, all trying to describe this larger source of energy, but they are desperately inadequate. No matter what they call it, most people in the world agree that there is a creative source greater than we are. (Even atheists admit there are phenomena they can't explain.)

In a book I use with clients called *The Greatest Salesman in the World*, the author, Og Mandino, explains how even our physical bodies *prove* our connection with this infinite source of energy. He writes, "Move your hand in haste before another's eyes and his eyelids will blink. Tap another on his knee and his leg will jump. Confront another with dark horror and his mouth will say, 'My God' from the same deep impulse. My life need not be filled with religion in order for me to recognize this greatest mystery of nature." I find this undeniable connection we share with the source of energy that created everything in the entire Universe astonishing and inspiring.

Let me illustrate this woo-woo concept for you in another way. Imagine that each of us is like a unique musical instrument designed by our creator to make a particular tone or sound. Just as an instrument is created to make a particular sound in an orchestra or band, we each were crafted to serve the world in which we live in a unique way. Maybe I was created to make the light, fluttering notes of a flute; maybe you provide the consistent deep tones of a trombone. No instrument sounds exactly like another. In addition, no instrument creates any sound without the breath from its player flowing through it. The musician chooses which buttons to push in order to create certain sounds and also determines the volume and pace of the sound that comes out.

Similarly, when we allow the energy of the Universe to flow through our gifts and out into the world—goodness gracious, does it ever make the most beautiful, unique sound!

Here is an example of what this looks like in the real world. I was doing some work with a roofing and siding company recently, and as a part of the workshop, I interviewed the five supervisors in front of the entire team. The first question I asked each of them was how they came to work in construction. One of the foremen started his answer to my question with this statement: "I think I knew I would work in construction the first time I built a home for my pet pigeons." In an instant, the entire room of brawny construction guys who had been only moderately paying attention to the presentation up to this point stopped moving and leaned in almost simultaneously. Pet pigeons? We need some more information please! With the help of some encouraging questions, the supervisor told us all about how growing up, he had loved pigeons. He and his friends would climb up into the rafters under bridges and take the chicks (only those that already had feathers and could survive, he clarified) from the pigeon nests, bring them home, and tame them. This gruff, blue collar tough guy came alive before our very eyes as he spoke. He told us about how he had taken some old sheets of plywood from his uncle's garage and built a special, if imperfect, cage in his bedroom for his birds.

Yes, we were talking about his work, but we were talking about something bigger too. While he didn't say it in these words, the combination of his love for these pets and construction felt like his point of connection to the greater source. Everyone in the room could *feel* it. When we are in the presence of someone as the energy of the Universe flows through their unique gifts and out into the world, we can *feel* it. Even when they are just talking about the experience; it's that vivid. No one in that room will ever forget that conversation, especially me.

Here's another example. As a part of my business with Amy Kemp, Inc., I do two weekend events each year. One is called Pause and the other Refresh. Refresh was inspired by my friend Alison and our shared love for the trips we had earned while leading large organizations in direct sales. For one week each year on these incentive trips, we gathered with other top leaders in the company in the most incredible locations around the world—England, Italy, Germany, China, Hawaii, and more. There were only a few hours of meetings the whole week. The rest of our time was filled with unforgettable travel experiences—meals shared on the Great Wall of China, rides in the London Eye, tours of St. Peter's Basilica in Vatican City, and even ziplining adventures above the lush rainforests of Maui.

On those trips, conversations would happen among the leaders and their spouses about systems we used to make our homes run more efficiently, books we were reading, business coaches we were working with, and of course we shared lots of stories and lessons learned from our business experiences. These conversations and the friendships forged through shared trips around the world impacted my business more than any training event I ever attended. Alison and I wanted to create this same experience for other women, and because she owns an incredible luxury travel business, she and I partner to take twenty women to a different city each year for a long weekend of connection and fun. We hosted our first weekend in our home city of Chicago, then we traveled to San Antonio, and next year we are going to Sedona.

If you want to experience the flow of source energy through a person, you should see Alison describing, preparing for, or in the throes of any incredible travel experience. Our good friend Jamie says, "Everyone should experience Alison high on travel at least once in their lifetime." There is something about curating unforgettable experiences in places around the world that opens Alison up to this flow of energy through her and out into the world. It's magnetic and inspiring to watch as she overflows with enthusiasm. She could invite me to go anywhere in the world that she planned, and without even much explanation of where we were going,

What if everything
we want and are trying
to create depends
on the strength of
our connection to the
source from which
all things came?

I'd hand her my credit card and follow willingly. Bringing Alison's woo-woo energy to Amy Kemp, Inc. has been such a valuable addition to my offerings as a coach.

On the Edge of Completely Bananas

While I believe using our unique gifts to serve the world is what we were created to do, the experience of it can feel vulnerable and scary at times. I asked a couple who have been my one-on-one clients for the past year about this feeling. Don and Liz recently moved their family from a "normal" suburban life where they had two full-time traditional jobs to a rural farm property from which they now collect eggs, raise chickens, and grow much of their own food. Liz is leading and growing a home school co-op while also using her doctorate in physical therapy to help people heal their bodies holistically. When we had this conversation, they were in the midst of moving to a new farm property that they found through the craziest, most unreal set of connections—it sort of "fell into their laps" (which happens a lot when you are connected to the source). I asked them, "What does it feel like to be completely in the flow of the Holy Spirit?" (Their faith is Christian, so this is the term they use to describe this energy.)

Don, who tends to be very analytical, practical, and dry in his delivery, surprised me when he paused and said, "It feels like we are living just on the edge of completely bananas." I about fell out of my chair! *On the edge of completely bananas!* I couldn't possibly love this description any more! While it is exhilarating and exciting, when the same energy that created the Universe is moving through you in very real ways, it can take your breath away!

Liz described some of the benefits of living in a constant state of faith that the next steps will appear when it's time to take them. She explained, "We have found peace in our lives. We've gained clarity. We've been able to slowly remove things from our lives that weren't serving us to allow for more of what contributes positively to our family vision. Don and I have grown closer than we've ever been." Almost everyone I know who is living "on the edge of completely bananas," like Liz and Don, also says that living in this flow of energy provides an overwhelming and constant sense of peace. This is one of the best parts of living in the woo-woo.

When Woo-Woo Happens, You Know It

In addition, when we open ourselves to this flow, things happen that are bigger and more astonishing than we could ever imagine or create on our own. There is a video on YouTube called *"The Greatest Showman*—The Story Behind the Making of the Movie"* that has been watched almost a hundred million times, and maybe even more by the time you read these words. (I'm not at all ashamed to tell you that perhaps ten thousand of those views are mine!) I encourage you to find it and watch it.

The video starts with an interview of Keala Settle, the actress playing Lettie Lutz, and Michael Gracey, the director of the hit movie *The Greatest Showman*. They set the stage in this interview, explaining that the song "This Is Me" had just been written and the cast was going to perform it for the first time in front of potential investors. This performance could determine whether the film would get green-lit and become a movie or not. Gracey says, "We knew that this would be the anthem of the film, but no one had heard it before. And no one had heard Keala sing it. And Keala... didn't even want to come out from behind the music stand." In fact, he encourages her before the performance begins to "step out into the ring, metaphorically" as the movie is all about the origins of the circus.

In the end, Settle describes the performance as "otherworldly," and Gracey says, "It was one of those moments that will stay with me for the rest of my life, and fortunately, we filmed it."

What happens in those four minutes must be experienced to be fully appreciated. It is raw and vulnerable, and after you watch the video, you'll probably share it with a few friends as well. On that fated day, the energy of the Universe really did move through Settle and the other performers as they sang. The private backstage performance continues to reverberate and impact people around the world today.

One lesson I learned from this video is that we get to experience the flow of universal energy even more robustly when we are connected with other people. We are designed to live and create in community. When Settle starts singing at the very beginning, her voice is quiet, shaky, and even off-pitch. This is not a perfect performance by any means. She is, in fact, physically standing behind a music stand. Slowly, she starts to walk into the middle of the room, but the power of the song doesn't really hit you until one of the backup singers stands up on the seat of his chair in the back row. Settle turns and faces this fellow performer head on, and she motions with her hand to have him sing the first lines of one of the verses. He sings the words with boldness and passion while looking straight into her eyes. Settle turns back around after this brief interaction with her peer and is transformed into a new singer. His boldness feeds her courage, and she opens herself to let the energy move through her at another level as she belts out the words to the chorus of the song!

About halfway through her performance, at a particularly tender moment in the song, Settle's voice waivers and fills with raw emotion. She walks over to Hugh Jackman, the famous leading actor and star of the show, whose eyes are now full of tears and whose face is red with emotion. Feeling her fear, he reaches out his hand, and she grabs it with her shaky hand, as if she is holding on for dear life. Reassured by this supportive gesture, she continues singing with renewed courage, and again the performance moves to a new level of impact and power. You see, even when the energy of the Universe is flowing through you, sometimes you get spooked in the middle and need to grab the hand of a friend and be reassured that you've got this.

I have reached out a shaky hand to a friend or mentor many times throughout the process of creating this book. Am I ready to write a book? Will people buy my book? Will the book serve the people it is written for? What if I invest all of this time and effort and it's a flop? Does this investment in creating this book make sense financially? So many people grabbed my hand in these moments of questioning and said in different ways, "It's time. Do this. You are worth the investment. People need you to create this resource." No worthy creation is made in a vacuum. This work, and others like it, is a collection of the energy of the Universe flowing through a community of people and connecting them together while they also are connected to the source of all things. What a miracle!

I realized another truth about this woo-woo phenomenon while watching this video: we don't get to pick if or when this flow casts our unique contribution out into the world with such power and scope that it changes everything. We

When I am open and
allow this limitless energy
to flow through me,
something magnificently
magical happens.

all have unique gifts, and we get to choose to practice using them mostly in unseen, even mundane spaces. We work on our craft and hone it through often-boring repetition, and then for some people at some point, the flow of the energy of the Universe moves through us and into the world in a way that resonates so much with other people, it multiplies our impact beyond anything we could have ever imagined.

By the time this fated session was recorded, Keala Settle had been singing for her whole life. For most of those hours of practice, very few people were listening. Then she began auditioning for roles in musicals, and her voice began to be heard by more and more people. She eventually landed several smaller parts in Broadway performances, then some larger ones until she finally landed this breakout role in the movie *The Greatest Showman*. When she performed the song at this closed presentation, she definitely didn't know this intimate behind-the-scenes performance would be watched millions and millions of times only by the luck of having been recorded at all. But in this moment, the energy of the Universe moved through her voice so mightily, it could not be contained. We don't get to pick those multiplying moments. They just happen.

Blocking the Flow

Next, let's talk about what blocks the flow of the energy of the Universe. Remember my first question in this chapter? What if our number one job in life is to simply allow powerful universal energy to flow through us and out into the world? If the answer to this question is yes, then I must ask the next question: What is keeping the flow of this powerful energy from moving through you?

As I've taught this concept to clients around the country in my online courses and in-person workshops, we have compiled a list of things that most people agree block this flow:

- unhealed emotional pain
- mistreatment of any kind or unhealthy relationships
- lackluster or missing boundaries
- exhaustion
- cheap "highs"—any addictive escape
- fear
- shame
- secrets
- comparison
- isolation or loneliness
- mental illness
- physical illness or pain
- limiting subconscious thought habits

I'm sure there are others as well, but if this is a good starting list, then I must ask another question. (Goodness, I really do *love* a great question!) If everything else stayed the same in your life and you just focused on one change that would open up the point of connection between you and the energy of the entire Universe, where would you *start*?

Can I recommend that you start by addressing your subconscious thought habits? After all, the core message of this entire book is that no matter how hard you may try, *you can't outwork your thought habits.*

Subconscious Thought Habits Can Block the Flow

Human beings all have two minds—a conscious mind and a subconscious mind. Most of us go through our lives swirling in our conscious thoughts, and we forget how astonishingly powerful the subconscious mind is. This subconscious mind is where our thought habits live. Many times, consciously recognizing the limiting thought habits that are creating blockage in our lives is all it takes to move us back into the flow of creation.

In his book *The Breakthrough Code*, Tom McCarthy writes, "The subconscious mind is everyone's superpower and secret weapon. While your conscious mind can process about forty bits of information per second, your subconscious mind can process forty million bits of information per second! Your subconscious mind can also tap into all of our collective minds, every brilliant thought that's ever been thought, or what is often called the Universal Life Force."

There is so much to learn about the subconscious mind and how to harness its power. I think of the subconscious mind as the door at the connecting point between us and the source of all energy. It acts as a conduit of this unlimited power. Unlike the conscious mind, the subconscious mind never sleeps, making it possible to apply energy to the achievement of our goals even while we sleep. It is also ravenously hungry for something to obsess about so it can apply its power to something useful. The best times to connect to the subconscious mind are in the morning right when we wake up and at night just before we fall asleep because our conscious minds are less likely to distract us then. It's also a good idea to check in with the subconscious mind several times a day if we want to create change in our lives more quickly.

How do we check in with the subconscious mind and harness its power? This deeper mind responds best to pictures and images while our conscious mind works more in words and numbers. It will work all day and night to create in the outside world what we show it in these images. In fact, most of what we have in front of us right now is a result of the instructions we have been giving our subconscious minds, whether we realize it or not. At any time, we can choose to provide it with a clearer image of what we want, and it will in turn provide better instructions we can follow to create those results. Again, the subconscious mind cannot magically provide the results we desire, but it can give us inspired ideas and we can choose to act on them.

Finally, the fuel that keeps the subconscious mind working is faith that what we are imagining and desiring will come to pass. The bigger the belief, the more power the subconscious mind can use to create the ideas needed to bring this desire into reality. It's like faith is the push that swings open the door between us and the power of the Universe. Without it, our thoughts have little power. Again, we don't have to know *how* to create what it is we want. We have to grow the belief that what we want is absolutely available to us. In this spirit of faith, we simply get to pay attention throughout our days and to act on inspired ideas when they show up.

The best part of living a life connected to source energy is that we can create so many of the things we've been longing for without strife or struggle. And when we create them by acting on the inspired ideas delivered to us through our subconscious minds, we get to learn once again that the whole process is not really even about the new thing—the new house, the increased income, the exciting romantic relationship—it's about the experience of that Universal life source flowing through us. It's magnificent. It's otherworldly. It's life-giving. It's bliss.

In closing, what if our number one job in life isn't to work really, *really* hard to create what we want (though certainly working at something is part of the process)? What if it's a little more woo-woo than that? What if our number one job is to take care of the point of connection between ourselves and the abundant power that created the Universe so that this power can flow through our unique gifts and out into the world? I believe it is.

CHAPTER 5 EXERCISE
DISCOVER YOUR HABITS OF THINKING

Take some time to reflect and then answer these questions in your journal.

- What if my number one job in life is to simply keep an open passageway through me so this powerful universal energy can flow through me and out into the world?

- How connected am I to the source from which all things come?

- What have I been designed to create or do that could serve the world in a specific way if I allow source energy to flow through me?

- What blockage is inhibiting the flow of this energy through me right now?

If you want to address once and for all the subconscious thought habits that are holding you back, check out my offerings at AmyKemp.com. This is exactly what I do with my clients.

6

Boundaries Protect You and Allow You to Grow

I N A famous scene from one of my all-time favorite movies, *Dirty Dancing*, the sultry, talented dance instructor and protagonist, Johnny, is teaching his new temporary partner, Baby, how to dance. He holds his arms out in a frame facing her and says, "This is my dance space. This is your dance space. I don't go into yours; you don't go into mine. You gotta hold the frame." I love this scene because it illustrates so perfectly what happens in a relationship between two people with healthy self-esteem and appropriate boundaries. I hold my space to live, you hold yours, and together we dance.

One of the least talked about and greatest casualties of low self-esteem in our world is the ability to let someone else believe differently than you do, to let them live differently or choose differently, without feeling threatened or without needing to force them into your own space or way of thinking. People with low self-esteem have an exceptionally hard time creating and keeping distinct boundaries in their lives, "holding their space," and they have an even harder time allowing others to do the same.

I can celebrate the tattoo on your shoulder and how much you love it without needing to get one on mine. I can admire your ability to walk into any room and meet every person there while only needing to meet two or three to have just as much fun. I can listen to your opposing perspective on controversial political issues and still respect you while holding my own views that are very different.

I can hold my space. You can hold your different, even opposing space. *And* we can dance.

Also, people with low self-esteem and who lack boundaries can usually only be in relationships with people who have the same beliefs they do because their ideas are so closely tied to their identity. They can't stand the disagreement, and without the needed boundaries, they can't tolerate any kind of challenge. It is too risky, too hard to tolerate, too awkward. Even worse, they often hide or sacrifice their beliefs at the altar of fitting in, being liked, or avoiding conflict. Today more than ever before, we often come face to face with our own insecurities through our relationships with others. If we don't know how to maintain healthy boundaries, relationships with people who believe differently than we do are impossible.

In his book *Today I Begin a New Life*, Dave Blanchard writes, "We know that 95 percent or more of the population cannot separate their ideas from their self-worth... We have two choices: We can either choose to be right, control, and crush [people], or we can choose to be rich—in both money and relationships!" What usually happens is that our ideas, opinions, and thoughts become so personal and so close to us, because we are thinking about them *all the time*, that when someone criticizes our idea, we feel this negative response deeply. When we are attached to our ideas, it becomes nearly impossible to receive helpful feedback. Therefore, if we want to create more impact and income, we have to first create a boundary between our feeling of value and our ideas.

Let me give you a simple picture of what this can look like in a real-life work setting. My husband, Ryan, is an assistant principal at a high school. This year, he talked to me a *lot* about bus lanes. Yep, bus lanes. Every morning, when the buses come to the back of the school and drop off students, he is deeply bothered. He is a logistics/operations type of thinker, and when he sees inefficiency or danger in a process in the school building, he wants to fix it. It's actually a very helpful trait in his role as an administrator. So, he had this idea to reconfigure the bus lanes because right now buses and cars are mixed in one line dropping off kids, and kids who drive to school are walking through the drop-off line to get into the school from their cars. It has driven him crazy for years.

Does he have a good idea? A valid idea? Has he been obsessing about it? Yes, yes, and *yes!*

The Idea Box

Now, let's play out a pretend scenario. This has not actually happened, but I'm imagining it as an example of the importance of having boundaries between our feelings of self-worth and our ideas. Let's say Ryan heads into a meeting with the leadership team at the school. He has finally worked on his idea enough and gotten frustrated enough with the status quo to present his plans for a change to the bus lanes.

In my mind, I see him holding a neatly wrapped box that represents the idea. His beloved "idea box" is in his hands, pressed very close to his chest, almost as if the box is physically a part of his body. I imagine my very tall husband walking into the boardroom and climbing his six-foot-four-inch frame up to sit on the long rectangular conference table surrounded by the entire leadership team, clutching the box at his heart. Again, he has thought about the idea in this box so much it feels as if it is literally a part of him, and the meeting begins.

He opens the lid to his box and passionately presents the idea to the room. The first person to speak after him responds with a question about whether the idea would slow traffic on the street in front of the school, causing a bigger issue. Another person, he notices, leans back with her arms crossed and glances at her watch, clearly not caring one bit about the bus lanes. A third person agrees, but hesitantly. Each time Ryan's idea gets poked and prodded and even disagreed with, he *feels* it. It is all very personal, as if they are poking and prodding *him*. He has *become* the idea, so the criticism feels like it is aimed at *him* rather than the idea itself.

Have you ever had this experience where you almost physically felt the pokes and prods of those around you as you presented an idea? Have you ever felt as if you were sitting on top of a table in a conference room being critiqued in front of your peers and leaders? If yes, the discomfort and pain you experienced in that moment resulted from a lack of adequate boundaries between you and your idea. In your mind, you *became* your idea.

What if, instead of the idea being attached to Ryan, to his self-worth, he walked into that same meeting carrying the same "idea box" in his backpack? What if he sat down, pulled the idea out of the backpack, and placed it in the middle of the table while staying seated in his chair with the rest of the team? This idea is not him. It is separate from him. He can put it out on the table, and it can be questioned and poked and prodded; heck, he may even take a few stabs at it himself. He will not be offended or feel attacked. No one is criticizing him personally. Everyone can even agree to disagree on this idea, and it has no impact on their relationships. Together, they are looking at an idea, not at Ryan himself.

I'm guessing you've never considered boundaries from this angle.

Unfortunately, this kind of healthy conversation about ideas, where people don't take feedback personally, is extremely rare. It never happens without a leader setting the stage for the conversation and *constantly* reminding people that they are not their ideas. High-functioning teams invest a lot of time and money understanding these types of concepts so that they can have clear and accurate conversations that benefit the entire business or organization. When a team can openly and objectively discuss ideas without being attached to them, they become astonishingly effective.

Taking this a step further and into a more personal realm, is it possible to care deeply about a person, yet vehemently disagree with what they are saying or posting online? Can I sit over a meal or a cup of coffee with someone whose ballot was the opposite of my own and cultivate a meaningful friendship anyhow? What if what the people around me are saying or doing isn't *right* (according to my story, my perspective, my upbringing, my culture, or my faith)? Can I believe differently and still be someone's friend? Can I listen without needing to validate my own opinions and perspective? Is my self-esteem strong enough to celebrate the differences or at the very least *allow* them, or do I find myself retreating to relationships with people whose perspectives align with my own in order to feel comfortable?

The challenge is essentially the same one Johnny gave to Baby in *Dirty Dancing*. Can you hold your space, believing what you choose, while allowing me to hold mine, a space that is perhaps totally different than yours? Yes, but only if you have healthy boundaries. When we feel safe because of our boundaries, when we surrender our own need to be right, when we listen, when we step toward those who are different and maybe even grab hold of their hand, we can create a beautiful new dance, one of difference and diversity and strength.

Boundaries Spectrum

I can't dig deeply into the tender topic of boundaries without first pausing to acknowledge my own personal level of privilege. I don't just *have* privilege as a white, straight, wealthy, cis, college-educated woman, I fairly swim in it. I'll borrow the poignant words Melissa Urban uses in her *Book of Boundaries* when she writes, "Those privileges and that power mean I can speak a boundary with relative confidence, and generally expect others to respect my wishes. People who belong to historically marginalized groups—whether people of color, disabled, plus-sized, or LGBTQ+—don't have the same privilege, the same power, or the same relationship to boundaries that I do. Without that privilege, you're likely more fearful of setting a boundary and the truth is, others are less likely to respect it."

There *are* situations in which creating a new healthier boundary may not be accessible to people. Unfortunately, this is real, and changing this reality is excruciatingly slow. Take what you can from these chapters on boundaries, and I hope you can accept this humble acknowledgment as you read, knowing that your situation and level of privilege may not allow you to be as bold or as clear as mine does.

For decades, I have worked with women who struggle to create and hold healthy boundaries or, as Johnny would say in one of his dance lessons with Baby, to protect "their space" in their lives. Working as a coach, particularly with one-on-one clients with whom I meet for six or seven consecutive months, I have gotten an even closer view of how deeply boundaries impact women. Some of the patterns I see are tragically commonplace, yet the women immersed in them are almost uniformly unaware of what is happening. In order to help them understand what I was seeing and what they were experiencing, I created a continuum that I call the Boundaries Spectrum.

BOUNDARIES SPECTRUM

No Boundaries   Boundaries   Walls

I want to teach this to you just as I would teach it to a client in a one-on-one coaching session. Grab a blank piece of paper and draw a straight line that spans horizontally from one side to the other. Above it, I want you to write the words *Boundaries Spectrum*. The line you've drawn represents the full array of life experiences created by our boundaries. Now, draw three dots that sit on the line: one on the far-left side, one directly in the middle, and one on the right.

Under the dot on the far left side of the line, I want you to write the words *No Boundaries*. This dot represents the experience of women for whom there are very few or no boundaries. Women living life without the protection of boundaries work more hours than they are paid for, allow people to take advantage of their willingness to help, and the word *no* does not exist in their vocabulary unless they are saying it to themselves. They make decisions based on what is best for everyone else, usually not even considering themselves or their own needs in the process. They are paralyzed at the thought of being criticized or rejected and have a constant need for approval and reassurance from others. They frequently agree to do things they don't really want to do, and they often give beyond their resources, loaning money or helping people out of obligation or guilt, even when they are broke, exhausted, or physically worn down.

I asked some of my clients who have lived this way to share what it looks like in their lives to operate with few to no boundaries, and here are some examples they gave me:

- "I let people take my time with unannounced visits, requests for rides, or last-minute errands, even when I have plans for something else (particularly things for myself)."

- "I said yes to helping my friends move even though I knew that my back would be sore, and I would pay for the heavy lifting for the next week."

- "I don't say or do anything when my sister's kids (who are adults and still act like middle schoolers) erupt like emotional toddlers at family dinners and mistreat my sister in front of everyone."

- "I agree to be on call on my day off because I'm afraid to say no and inconvenience the other people I work with who have small children."

- "I fill my calendar with meetings, so I never have time to *actually* work, then I frequently have to work when I don't want to, on the weekend or in the evening."

- "I give in to subtle jabs and socially drink at work functions to fit in even when I don't want to."

Having no boundaries is painful. Clients who have lived in this state for years often feel powerless and full of rage and

We can't stifle
our intuition in one
area of life, then
have access to it
in every other.

resentment, and they can wind up coping with these intense emotions in self-destructive ways.

Next, let's look at the other side of the Boundaries Spectrum. On the far right side of the line you drew on your paper, I want you to write the word *Walls*. The opposite of living a life with no boundaries is living a life behind walls. Living behind walls looks like fierce independence, constant fear that someone might see the real you, anxiety in social settings where people are being honest and vulnerable, and very few, if any, truly intimate relationships in your life. Interestingly, many women who live behind walls are often very social, engaging, and funny, but they know how to deflect and exit quickly when the conversation gets too personal. They are essentially hiding in plain sight. Also, while everyone *thinks* they know this person, when pressed, they really don't know much about them at all. Emotional walls like these can protect women from harmful or abusive relationships, but it's lonely and exhausting to keep holding them up. They also end up keeping out the helpful, nurturing relationships these women crave.

I asked my clients who have lived life behind thick walls to describe this experience, and here is what they shared:

- "Not only did I have no help with household chores, but I was also terrified to ask anyone to help me for fear they would be in my home and see the real me. Very few people get to see her."

- "The few times I felt comfortable enough to open up with potential new friends, I was so desperate for connection, I overshared, and they quietly pulled away. I thought this was because they didn't like me or I was too much for them, but actually, it was my desperation and oversharing that pushed them away. I couldn't ease into the relationship."

- "I was super rigid about my employees following the rules exactly, not considering the complexity of their lives. I lost some great people in my attempts to control everything and everyone."

- "I was constantly on the lookout for people who were trying to 'get me' or take advantage of me. My hypervigilance kept me from relationships with so many people who could have helped me grow my business."

- "Because I couldn't show myself fully to anyone, people just seemed like objects to be manipulated and moved around. I couldn't let myself get too close. I was so lonely."

Those who live behind thick walls have very few people who *really* know them, even though they may be the life of the party and have gobs of acquaintances. They can be demanding at home and in work settings, doing whatever it takes to get ahead and to keep people at a distance. They do not share their fears or their insecurities with anyone. They also quickly cut people out of their lives once they have stopped serving a purpose or if they question them in any way. They have a hard time delegating tasks or trusting others to help them. They often work an extraordinary number of hours in order to prove themselves or to avoid criticism or failure.

So, we've covered the two extreme ends of the Boundaries Spectrum—*no boundaries* and *walls*. Now, in the center dot on the line on your paper, I want you to write the words *Healthy Boundaries*. Boundaries exist in the life experience between having no protection or limitations and having thick walls. Walls keep bad things out, but they keep good things out too. Living with no boundaries lets *everything* in, without offering any kind of protection. Healthy boundaries keep bad things out, but they let the good things in. Over the years, I have collected a few different definitions of boundaries that I really like. Here are a few:

- From Brené Brown's bestselling *Dare to Lead*, boundaries are "making clear what's okay and what's not okay, and why."

- In Melissa Urban's *Book of Boundaries*, they are "clear limits you establish around the ways you allow people to engage with you, so that you can keep yourself and your relationships safe and healthy."

- Author and therapist Nedra Glover Tawwab says "boundaries are the gateway to healthy relationships." Think about that. You simply *cannot* have a healthy relationship with anyone or anything without a healthy boundary.

- In Dr. Henry Cloud and Dr. John Townsend's bestselling book, *Boundaries: When to Say Yes, How to Say No to Take Control of Your Life*, they write, "Boundaries define us. They define *what is me* and *what is not me*. A boundary shows me where I end and someone else begins, leading me to a sense of ownership... In short, boundaries help us keep the good in and the bad out."

- And, in what is perhaps my favorite definition of them all, Prentis Hemphill says, "Boundaries are the distance at which I can love you and me simultaneously."

In Heather Plett's outstanding book *The Art of Holding Space*, I found a helpful image of what having healthy relational boundaries should look like. Plett uses a picture of a cell to represent a person in a relationship. Healthy boundaries are the membrane that surrounds the cell. One of the reasons I love this image so much is that a cell is protected by a permeable membrane and not a solid, impenetrable wall.

The membrane can bend, adapt, move, and change, allowing nutrients in and keeping out disease or other potentially harmful intruders. Like cells, we are fluid, changing beings, and we do need real connection, authentic relationships, and other people in order to be at our best. We need to let things in if we want to survive and thrive, and we need to keep out things that are hurtful and damaging. Boundaries in our lives can be permeable but still protective, not rigid and unyielding.

Living a life with healthy boundaries is full of freedom and peace. People with appropriate boundaries are clear about their values, and they can say no to things that don't fit with their priorities without needing to explain why or justify their choices. They tend to listen to their intuition, looking inside to make decisions and not to other people. They work hard, but not to the point of exhaustion and overwhelm. They ask for and receive help at work and at home, and they protect time for exercise, sleep, and recreation. They also have safe relationships within which they can be vulnerable, and they can gauge how much is appropriate to share within these relationships. Living with boundaries is a daily practice, not a destination.

All of this begs the question, How do you know whether you are living behind thick impenetrable walls, lacking boundaries altogether, or if you have healthy boundaries? The answer is quite simple. You ask this really important question: *What is motivating you to create the protection you feel you need?* If your protection is motivated by fear, extreme self-protection, defensiveness, shame, or secrets you don't want anyone to know, then it is most likely a wall. The creation of boundaries, on the other hand, is motivated by healthy, healed self-esteem. Basically, you love yourself enough to demand that you are treated with respect by all

Boundaries are not mean. Our deeply ingrained cultural conditioning wants to tell us they are.

people. Healthy, healed self-esteem says to the world, "I'm okay disappointing people. I'm not responsible for other people's emotions or responses. I'm not nervous this inter-action will destroy our relationship because I don't *need* the relationship. I am not afraid of being abandoned. I under-stand my own needs; I am in tune with them. I deserve to be treated with kindness and respect."

What motivated my creation of the Boundaries Spec-trum was this realization: the experiences of having thick high walls and of having no boundaries are eerily similar. It's not uncommon for people to vacillate between those two extremes in different parts of their lives. I see very successful clients do this all the time. They are fiercely independent and absolutely *in charge* at work, putting in long hours, taking on the most challenging projects, and volunteering for every opportunity presented. They lead meetings with confidence, they make difficult decisions without hesitation, they enforce rules and policies, and they hold people accountable for their behavior and their performance. They put the majority of their best energy into the space where they feel the safest emotionally—work. They have few friends, and they don't appear to care or need them.

These same women who are beasts in the boardroom can become completely different people in the context of personal relationships, with family members or in their dating lives, partnerships, or marriages. At home, they become meek and powerless and have no boundaries. The difference between those two spaces? There are thick walls and no emotional intimacy at work, and they use power to keep more intimate relationships at bay. In spaces where intimacy is required, they feel unsafe, exposed, and even desperate for love and belonging. This fear causes them to accept mistreatment, to take responsibility for things that they shouldn't, and to accommodate everyone else before taking care of themselves.

It's almost as if the ends of the Boundaries Spectrum line you drew on your paper have been bent into a circle and connected, blending the two experiences into one. In fact, on your piece of paper where you have drawn the Boundaries Spectrum, I want you to go ahead and draw a circle underneath it. Inside the circle, write the words *No Boundaries=Thick Walls.*

I have observed clients living with no boundaries in some spaces and living behind thick walls in others, and they all share a similar emotional experience. Here is how they describe it:

- **Isolation:** Even when surrounded by people, few people actually see you or know you.

- **Fear:** You live in paralyzing fear that if people *really* knew you or your life circumstances, their opinions of you would change drastically. You become whoever you need to be in spaces where you have few or no boundaries, and you hide emotionally in spaces where you have thick walls.

- **Overwhelm:** In both situations, you don't have anyone but yourself to depend on to get things done. You often carry the weight of both home and work alone and may even say yes to volunteer opportunities that add to the load you carry. The weight of all your obligations is nearly unbearable.

- **Resentment or Anger:** In every setting, your needs are the last priority. No one notices or cares that you are sacrificing yourself completely, and over time, you grow angry and bitter. To you, people seem self-absorbed and inconsiderate.

Whether you are living with no boundaries or behind thick walls, I want to invite you to observe yourself without harsh judgment or condemnation. Almost always your choices have been a result of circumstances that were out of your control; you made choices to protect yourself as best as you could. You were doing the best you could with what you knew at the time. I also invite you to be curious and to question whether these protective measures have become more harmful than helpful as you have grown and changed.

Our Intuition Is an Internal Boundaries Radar System

Before we can begin to create better boundaries in our lives, we need language that can describe our experiences. When we can accurately name what is happening in our relationships with people and our work, we can start to make better choices. Let's start by talking about the role intuition plays in boundary-setting.

A client of mine was raised by a mom who struggled with addiction and mental illness, and her struggles created a volatile, unpredictable environment at home. Most of the time, even in her earliest memories, my client was more of a parent to her mom than vice versa, carrying an unfair burden of parenting and managing adult responsibilities in her home and with her siblings. As a teenager, she was the one who made sure there was a Christmas tree up and gifts under it every December. She made sure all the bills were paid on time and that her younger siblings' birthdays were celebrated. Until she moved out at the age of eighteen, my client's intuition frequently said to her, "This isn't right. I shouldn't have to do this." However, she had to ignore this gut feeling in order to survive and care for her family. Also, to her credit, with grit and determination, she managed the weight of these adult roles exceptionally well.

Fast-forward with me about twenty-five years to today as my client is building a successful business. Some of the skills she learned from growing up so quickly serve her well as an entrepreneur. She is resourceful, can solve about any problem, and can read people and their emotions with amazing accuracy, a skill she most likely honed during years of having to intuit her mom's almost unpredictable moods and binges. However, the quiet voice of intuition that said "This isn't right" over and over, which she ignored in order to survive growing up, can be difficult to access in her adult life, and this has caused some real challenges. How available does she need to be for her clients, and is she responsible for managing their emotions? Does she need to answer calls immediately? On weekends? Holidays? How many hours a week is appropriate for her to work? Why is it so easy for her to fall into the unsustainable habit of working to exhaustion, coming home many nights well after supper? I would argue that the internal guidance system that helps us make these kinds of choices about what is acceptable and what isn't is there; she just doesn't always hear or trust it.

Again, here's the tragic loss in situations like this. When you silence the intuitive voice inside you that says "This is too much for me; I am not responsible for this" for long enough, you lose access to it not only in the environment where you need it to survive, you lose access to it *everywhere*. When you don't listen to that little whisper inside you that knows what is okay and what isn't for long enough, you cut off your access to that voice in all areas, not just in one relationship or situation. Again, there is absolutely no judgment attached to this observation, only compassionate understanding. My client did what she had to do to survive. She was brave and resourceful, and it's actually miraculous that she overcame as many obstacles as she did.

It's just that *you can't stifle your intuition in one area of life, then have access to it in every other.* When our boundaries are repeatedly violated by people in our lives, and we stifle our intuition in order to survive the inappropriate breach, we learn to ignore that intuitive feeling, our body's internal boundaries radar system, in every area of our lives.

Two Areas of Struggle for Women

I see this show up most frequently in two areas of boundaries with my female clients. First, so many women have dysfunctional relationships with food. I can't help but connect this to a lack of trust of our internal guidance systems. Our intuition is what tells us when we are hungry and when we are full. It tells us when we crave something specific that our body needs for energy or nutrition or maybe just for enjoyment. But when we have ignored that intuitive connection with our bodies in one area, we can't just reawaken it instantly when we sit down to eat.

We may overeat because we aren't in touch with ourselves enough to know we are full. Or we undereat because we don't listen to the cues our body gives us saying we are hungry. We don't trust ourselves with food because we don't trust our intuition, so every bite we eat becomes a decision for our already overworked brains. This cycle is exhausting. It doesn't help that our society has an entire value system for women but not men on this issue. As my friend and personal guide in the area of body image, eating psychology coach

Emily LaVoie reminds us, "Food is meant to be enjoyed, not feared. Even if we all ate the same and exercised the same, we would still all look different. We all deserve more than a life spent trying to shrink our bodies. You are not alive to shrink your body until you die." Women are wasting hours of energy worrying that the shapes and sizes of our bodies don't match some idealized and unrealistic model while men are connecting with people, growing their businesses, and working to create all the things we also want—income, impact, and influence. If we could recapture all of the energy women spend making decisions about food and then feeling guilty or regretting those decisions, and if we could direct it toward something constructive, I believe we could solve many of our world's most challenging problems.

The second area where our lack of access to intuition plagues women is in our dysfunctional relationships with our work. Our intuition is what tells us when we are worn out and need a break or when we need to be done working for the day. When we continuously push through these quiet feelings and keep working, we eventually pay the price. So many women end up in a constant cycle of overworking, getting burned out, exhausted, or sick and then having to take time off to recover. Pushing ourselves to the point of collapse isn't beneficial for any business or career. Let's pause and acknowledge that at the root of this vicious cycle is women not paying attention to or trusting the intuition inside of us that tells us to rest and replenish.

One of my clients, who worked for almost three decades building and leading an enormous nonprofit organization while largely ignoring her own needs, suffered a heart attack in her fifties. The worst part is that she didn't even *know* she'd had one until years later when she went to the hospital for something else. After running a battery of tests, the emergency room doctors asked when she had had "her heart attack." Shocked, she responded that she'd never had one. But tests and medical evidence showed that she most certainly had. Offhandedly, she then sighed and said to me some of the most haunting words I have ever heard in my life: "I guess this is common; women have silent heart attacks all the time."

Here are some other examples from client conversations of what it sounds like when women lose trust in their intuition:

- "Working twelve-hour days every week doesn't feel sustainable and leaves me with no energy for my family at home, *but* I just got promoted, the entire leadership team works at this pace, and I don't want to fall behind or not pull my weight."

- "I don't think my mom should be telling me this about my dad, *but* she seems to need me, and she is my mom."

- "I don't like when he makes crass jokes about women, *but* everyone at the meeting laughs like it's no big deal so I'm just going to laugh too."

- "I really don't want a glass of wine because it gives me a headache, *but* everyone else is drinking, so I'll just have one to fit in."

- "My dad's presence in my home doesn't feel safe. He drinks too much and gets loud and domineering. *But* he and my husband love to watch football together, and I don't want to take that time together away from either of them."

- "I don't like the tone of voice that employee uses, *but* she is the only one on our team who understands our scheduling software and we cannot afford to lose her, so I guess I'll just take it."

- "I am swamped with the amount of work I have already been assigned, *but* when the big boss asks, I just have to say yes."

Do you hear the repression of the quiet intuitive whisper inside of these statements? *This doesn't feel right* (pay close attention: *this* is your intuition!), but *I'm not sure so I'll just ignore it. My gut says one thing,* but *maybe I'm wrong? I probably shouldn't pay attention to that instinctual response. After all, the needs of others are more important than my own. I'll just push that feeling down, throw it to the side, trust someone else's take on it, or ignore it all together.*

When we lose touch with that instinctive feeling, important boundaries are often violated, and we allow others to determine what is okay and isn't in their treatment of us.

Reconnecting with Your Intuition

My company, Amy Kemp, Inc., exists to give people a safe space where they can begin to reconnect with their intuition. My group and one-on-one coaching engagements allow women to vent and *not* be okay, to express what they know in their gut to be true but have ignored for so long. Oftentimes, my one-on-one clients will sheepishly say to me, "You're the first person I've ever told that. It felt so good to say it out loud. I feel so much better already."

Many of these women hold important leadership roles and know that sharing their own personal struggles intimately with those they lead isn't appropriate. You cannot ask someone to hold an intimate personal space for you and then turn around and give clear or difficult feedback on their performance the next day. These leaders also can't always

The presence of
resentment almost
always signifies
the absence of a
needed boundary.

confide in family members or friends who may not really understand their work or unique leadership challenges, but they desperately need a space where they can share without fear or filters. Frankly, I don't want any leader to be lacking that kind of safe space in their lives. Everyone needs a place where she can *not* be okay safely.

For most people, this kind of safe space is usually created by a coach, a therapist, or a mentor outside of their work or family. I work with a coach personally because I need someone to hold space for me so that I have the energy I need to hold space for all of my clients. Again, people who are able to listen to your stories without attachment have most likely done a lot of work on their own personal growth, and they won't be overwhelmed by the intensity of your feelings or experiences.

I want to challenge you to pause and evaluate your life right now. Who knows how you are *really* doing? Is there anyone with whom you can be totally transparent and who has no attachment to the outcomes of your decisions? Who is supporting and holding space for you? If there is no one, stop everything you are doing and pursue this kind of support no matter what it takes. Do not *ever* apologize for investing a consistent, significant portion of your budget to pay someone to support you, and don't you dare for a second think that investment is selfish. It is the greatest gift you can give to yourself, to those who follow you, and to those you love.

Boundaries Are Not Mean

I want to shout an important message about the topic of boundaries from the rooftops for all of you to hear: *boundaries are not mean.* Our deeply ingrained cultural conditioning wants to tell us they are, especially or perhaps only for women. So many of the messages we receive as young girls and women tell us that communicating what we need clearly, disappointing people when we say no, knowing the limits of our giving, and not accepting harmful or hurtful behavior is *mean*. But setting a necessary boundary is the furthest thing from mean; it's actually the most accurate way to love and care for people, including yourself. It is not mean to create boundaries that protect you.

I've come to realize that what's actually mean is the outcomes of boundaries we *don't* set. Even worse, the person you are being mean to most when you don't set boundaries is *you*. It's mean to you to allow someone to mistreat you. It's mean to you to not express your needs, and then it's mean to others when you completely blow up later because you're so frustrated, and mean again when you feel guilty because of it! It's mean to you to say yes when you want to say no and then meaner still to be resentful and ugly to someone else later because you're so frustrated. It's mean to you and those you could serve with your unique gifts when you let yourself get run-down, exhausted, and sick. It's mean to not be available to your spouse, partner, or family because you've saved your availability for everyone else. *It is not mean to set healthy boundaries.*

Another one of my clients, whom I'll call Melissa for the sake of privacy, just created some life-changing boundaries with her ex-husband because of behavior she felt was intrusive and narcissistic. Though they have been divorced for years, they still share the parenting of their son, which requires regular communication. Her ex-husband had a habit of sending constant, urgent text messages, unexpectedly dropping by her place of work, and interrupting her with emails and phone calls throughout the week. Not only was this disruptive, but it also caused her to experience micro-bursts of trauma over and over and over. He did not deserve this level of access to Melissa.

Together, we came up with two simple boundaries for her communication with him. First, she is never to talk with him one-on-one, not even over the phone or via text. Narcissists are masterful at creating confusion, and she would often leave their conversations feeling uncertain and defeated. All communication with him should come through email and should always include her current husband. Second, they only speak live once a week and at a scheduled time when Melissa's husband is present.

These two simple boundaries have been life-changing. It took some time and repeated reminders to change his communication patterns, but she says that since making these changes, she feels more clear, confident, and peaceful. Freeing up this emotional energy has allowed her to close a business that had outlived its purpose, pursue a creative passion she had set down for decades, and begin writing her first book. When her ex-husband pushes on the boundaries, she simply reminds him that they will talk about whatever it is he wants to bring up on their next scheduled call. She does not respond to any texts, emails, or phone calls outside of that time. Some people do not deserve unlimited access to you.

Once again, I'd like to reiterate that boundaries are not mean. Boundaries are not mean. Boundaries are not mean. And can I mention just one more time that boundaries are *not* mean? Healthy boundaries aren't selfish or cruel, and they aren't about keeping *all* people out. They're about maintaining the energy, strength, and emotional stamina we need to show up at our best in the healthy relationships in our lives and protecting ourselves from those that harm us. In case you need to hear it one final time, boundaries are not mean.

CHAPTER 6 EXERCISE
RESENTMENT AUDIT

The presence of resentment almost always signifies the absence of a needed boundary. In an effort to strengthen or create needed boundaries, I want to challenge you to do what I call a Resentment Audit. Make a list throughout the next week of all of the spaces where you feel resentment. When you feel resentful, first write down where you are and what is happening. Then imagine a flashing red neon sign above you that says *Missing Boundary* with an arrow pointing down at the situation.

These are a few areas where it is common to discover resentment:

Work
- the number of hours you are working
- the workload you carry compared to your peers
- leaders who aren't communicating expectations
- being underpaid for your contributions

Marriage or partnership
- unmet expectations in your most intimate relationships
- tasks you are doing alone or without help
- inadequate time spent together or level of connection

Family
- the responsibility of preparing for events and celebrations
- care for elderly family members, babies, or small children
- time spent together—too much or not enough
- preparation of food, household chores not evenly distributed

At the end of the week, take some time to review your list. What new boundaries do you need to create to remedy each area where you feel resentment? What difficult conversations do you need to have? To whom do you need to say no? What obligations need to be unloaded from your list and given to someone else? Remember that it's okay to start with a tiny first step; setting boundaries is a lifelong daily practice, not a one-time action.

7

This Is Where I End and You Begin

L ET'S CONTINUE with the idea of boundaries but shift the focus to the way we lead others, set goals, and organize our daily schedules. Most people only talk about boundaries in the context of personal and professional relationships, and while these are vital, we also need boundaries in other spaces.

As I've better understood where I end and others begin, I have had to redefine my expectations of myself as I lead people. I have also had to learn that as a coach, I am not responsible for the experiences or outcomes of those with whom I work. I can journey alongside them, and the action *they* take as a result of my coaching can have a significant impact on their progress, but I cannot carry the weight of their burdens or feel like their failures and struggles are my fault. This separation between me and the results of other people is an important boundary if I want to increase my influence, impact, and income. Many women sabotage their growth, even turn down potentially life-changing leadership opportunities, because they don't have adequate boundaries here. The emotional weight of leading people is just too much to bear.

Maybe you can relate, and this is even why you've avoided pursuing the leadership roles within your company or chosen profession. Why would you want to apply for a leadership role where you would have to carry the feeling of *more* responsibility for others when just managing what you already have feels overwhelming? Even more, how can you really know and invest in people but not carry the pain of their challenges, failures, and choices? Can you sit back and watch someone struggle to succeed in a role that feels incredibly easy to you? How can you truly hold someone accountable to performing at a high level when you know what is happening in their life outside of work hours? Is it even possible to care but not *carry* the burdens of the people you have been entrusted to lead?

Allow me to take you back to the summer of 2012. My business was growing rapidly, and I was leading not only a large sales team, but also a growing team of leaders who were leading their own sales teams. If you had looked at the growth of the business from the outside, my business was thriving.

However, my *inside* experience was a different story. Inside, I was emotionally exhausted and wondering if I could handle the business getting any larger. Specifically, the challenge of leading leaders felt heavy and overwhelming. For some reason, I felt a higher level of responsibility for the success of my leaders than I did for my sales team. I often felt as if I was physically carrying the weight of their results on my shoulders.

Here are my words from a journal entry written in the middle of a year-long coaching engagement in which I was learning about my thought habits. I've changed all the names for privacy, but I wanted to share this entry because I think it illustrates the depth of my emotional attachment.

My talk with [one of my leaders] Tara went well yesterday. In fact, I felt great *after it. She walked herself through most of the obstacles, had a list of questions for me, and I was able to share my deep belief in her. This morning, whether it be from fatigue or whatever, I find my mind racing, wondering if I said too much, not enough, if I shouldn't have said this or that part and I realize that* all *of that worry and needing to be* perfect *in that conversation is a* problem. *It stems from the same fear, that her success/failure depends on me.*

My past experiences with Megan [another one of my leaders] could be another source of this fear. She is very talented and capable but has self-sabotaged for years. *Her business was thriving until she had a baby, had one of her key players quit, and ever since then, she doesn't engage with me, and she is barely holding on to her leadership position.*

It makes me feel so helpless watching her struggle, and I carry so much of that weight that I find myself unable to even make eye contact with her at times. Being in the same room with her takes my stress up ten notches. I rarely talk with her now because conversation seems futile. She doesn't follow through on things, there is a pervasive lack of discipline in all areas of her life, and she is unhealthy emotionally and physically. She has put herself into isolation mode.

The noise in my head is loud *on this one. I'm not going to give up on her, but I constantly wonder if there's some way I should be reaching out to her. However, I am the one allowing these unhealthy voices to be my guiding light here. I don't think that Megan's situation is my fault, yet because I'm so attached to the outcome, I've allowed it to make me feel that way. I* totally *am stopping myself from developing more leaders because of the repeated constant pain I feel when looking at my current leaders.*

Here is the thought habit that is at the root of this situation: the success/failure of my leaders is my responsibility.

What if I replaced it with this new thought: My leaders are independent, adult women who are responsible for the choices they make in building their businesses. They have great lessons to learn through the struggles they will face in growing their businesses.

I have learned that people don't need me to take responsibility for their successes or failures; they just need someone to listen without agenda or attachment. Plus, when I take on the experiences of others, I tend to shift into "fixing" mode, and anyone who has been on the receiving end of this kind of energy knows it doesn't feel good. No one wants to be fixed. Meanwhile, most of the time, after having been given a space in which they can process their emotions, the majority of people tend to move forward on their own. There is no need for me to carry another person's burden for them, especially when they feel completely better after a coaching conversation.

I recently read this amazing thought by Alan Cohen in his book *A Course in Miracles Made Easy*: "If you feel tired, fatigued or burned out after offering your service, you have forgotten that Higher Power is the real miracle worker. 'Why do I feel so tired after I do several healing sessions?' 'Because you think you are the healer.'"

People are not problems that need solving. They are not broken machinery that needs fixing. They are spiritual and emotional beings that need connection. Learning this has allowed me to hold space for more leaders and at a deeper, more meaningful level than ever before, and it has freed up energy and lessened the weight of taking on higher-level leadership roles.

People are not problems that need solving. They are spiritual and emotional beings that need connection.

Cutting the Ribbon

A coaching peer gifted me with another tool that has helped create a healthy emotional boundary between me and the leaders I serve. He learned it from a massage therapist friend who uses this to protect herself from the energy of those she serves with her hands.

I imagine that during a conversation with a client or someone I lead, the two of us are weaving a beautiful colored ribbon between us with our words, sort of like a braid. The fabric of our conversation is connecting us together layer after layer as I listen and as the person with whom I am talking shares. Each ribbon is as different as each conversation.

When the conversation ends, I often move my hands through the air as if I am cutting a ribbon with a pair of scissors. As I cut the imaginary ribbon, I say out loud to myself these simple but profound words: "What's mine is mine. What's yours is yours." I can cut the tie between us at the end of our conversation, letting my client leave with her portion of what we shared rather than turning our emotional connection into a tether that ties me to her experience and feelings for the rest of my day.

Stories We Tell Ourselves

In addition, at least once a week, and often as frequently as once a day in my conversations with clients, I say, "If you're going to make up a story, you might as well make up a good one." In other words, when something unexpected or disappointing happens in your life or work, you always get to decide how you interpret what just happened. There is a moment in which you get to decide what conclusion you will draw from that event, no matter how discouraged or power-less you feel in the moment. This, too, is a rarely recognized form of boundary we set between a circumstance and the impact it has on us. Something happens outside of our con-trol, *then* we get to respond to it. That little pause between the thing that happened and our response to it is critical. That pause is also a boundary.

I had an opportunity to practice this kind of bound-ary-holding recently after a conversation with a potential one-on-one coaching client. We had spoken at length about his story and the work I do, and he was enthusiastically ready to take on some of his limiting thought habits once and for all! He only needed to check in with his wife before making his final decision, but I felt confident after we talked that the answer would be a resounding yes.

I was busy the following day and didn't really think about following up, but two days later, I sent a quick email thanking him for his vulnerability in our conversation and asking if he was ready to order his materials and get started. He didn't respond that day, or the next. By the third day, the noise in my brain started to rev up a bit. I started to wonder if per-haps I had misread our conversation. Was the connection I felt one-sided? Was he not really interested in doing this work with me? Had my follow-up email been too strong or somehow offensive?

Two more days passed with no word, and then I got this email:

> Amy,
>
> Below is the amazing response that I sent last night . . . which . . . I sent to myself ☺ But nothing has changed since last night. Feedback and decision still stands! Was wondering why you hadn't replied. ☺ See email below!

> Amy,
>
> I thought about this more, prayed about it, and talked with my wife about it more. I'm in.
>
> You know between some of your commentary and material I have been reading over the last few days, I've even been stepping into a few meetings this week with a new perspective, and it has been amazing, refreshing, enjoyable. I feel like it's going to lead to good things. And it's rooted in all the same "already enough" mindset that we've been talking about.
>
> Would like some more of that and to make it permanent please! 😊
>
> And I very much like the "every three weeks" pace vibe. Sounds just right. 😊
>
> I'll look for the paperwork to get us started.
>
> Thanks—excited! 🙏

I had two thoughts upon reading this email. First, why don't I always listen to the advice I give to everyone else? I had been flirting with a story in my mind that wasn't serving me, that was causing me to doubt myself and my instincts about people. How much energy did I *waste* living in this story? How many more new clients had I missed as I was preoccupied with a story *that wasn't even true*?

Second, why did I automatically lean toward the negative story? It was *just as likely* that this prospective client had lost my email address or dropped his phone in the toilet or had an unexpected work trip come up, resulting in his lack of response. And those stories would have served me much more positively than the one I told myself.

Once again, I was reminded of this powerful lesson: *If you're going to tell yourself a story, you might as well tell yourself a good one.* Remember the pause—that tiny, deeply significant moment between what happened and the conclusion you decide you are going to draw from it? You get to choose. That, my friends, is a boundary. Use this kind of boundary to protect yourself from stories that don't serve you and wisely choose those that do.

Be Your Own Safe Space

When you have healthy boundaries, people can experience any kind of feeling in your presence without violating your boundaries. You can allow people to feel things intensely without needing to assuage their discomfort while also preventing their distress from harming you. I encounter this experience often in my role as a parent.

Our youngest son is a high energy, emotional being. When he feels something, he feels it intensely, and everyone around him knows it. At times, his anger or disappointment with a boundary (usually involving some sort of technology) affects how he treats me or the person in authority. Just the other day, when told it was time to shut off the television to get ready to go to a family gathering, he started a tirade that included some cruel words about what kind of a mom I am. I stopped him instantly and said, "You can kick and scream and be angry on the floor over there if you need to be. You can feel whatever you need to feel, but you will not mistreat me or speak to me disrespectfully because you are angry." Because I trust my boundaries and my ability to teach him how to treat me, I am not afraid of his emotions.

Protecting your own priorities is bound to upset those who benefitted most from your constant availability.

Let's transfer this kind of clarity to a work setting where, as a leader or business owner, you will be making decisions that certainly won't be popular with everyone they impact. If you cannot allow people to be upset and express their feelings while also being able to protect yourself from being mistreated, you'll most likely shy away from important decisions or difficult conversations. Even worse, you'll shy away from the pursuit of opportunities that create exactly what you want most—more income, influence, and impact.

In addition, people feel safer with those who have clear boundaries in their relationships. When they know where they stand and what is acceptable, they won't be worried about crossing a line. At the start of engagements with me, one-on-one clients will often preface a late-night text or early morning email with an apology: "I'm so sorry to bother you, but…" After some time, they stop apologizing because they learn that I won't *let* them bother me. I have healthy boundaries between my work and personal life that not only can be trusted by my family, but by my clients as well. My lack of constant availability enhances our relationship because they can trust my boundaries and know what to expect.

Set Goals That Acknowledge *All* Parts of Your Life

Next, I'd like to shift gears and draw attention to the relationships we have with our goals. I often see women return from an emotionally charged training session or event on fire and ready to take on the entire world. In a perfectly protected environment of inspiration and education, anything seems possible, and goals are set with *no* acknowledgment of life's realities, relationships with loved ones, or energy capacity. Ambitious women tend to be particularly challenged by this, and we want to return home and take off in a dead sprint. However, we often forget when we set these huge goals that we also have roles as moms or caretakers or partners that require a significant investment of energy and time. Please don't misunderstand. I have *chosen* my role as a mom, and it is my highest priority. The limitations this commitment places on my goals are limitations I embrace wholeheartedly. But in the throes of inspiration and excitement at an emotionally charged event, I tend to forget how much time and energy the role of being a mom actually takes.

You can set an ambitious goal at an event and chase after it; you just have to remember that going "all in" and working twelve-hour days doesn't go over very well when you also have babies, toddlers, or children of any age that you want to raise with intention and love. Again, I'm not saying events that promote dreaming or a fresh vision for the future are bad. I'm also not saying that you can't design a life with fewer caregiving responsibilities that need to be considered when pursuing your professional goals if you want, but if you are the one taking your aging parents to all of their medical appointments each week, this commitment has to be factored into the goal-setting process. Even if you feel deeply inspired, you might not have the luxury of letting your ambition charge ahead unchecked. Just as our successful relationships with people require boundaries, so do our relationships with our goals.

Here are some examples of goals with boundaries:

- I will increase my income by $20,000 this year while still taking off every Friday.

- I will add five new clients per month for the next three months while shutting my phone off by nine o'clock and taking a full day off each weekend.

- I will earn \$10,000 a month while spending three mornings a week with my mom at her assisted living home.

Goals without boundaries tend to lead to short periods of frenzied activity followed by exhaustion, burnout, sickness, and relational strife. Then when we pull back to recover from the frantic, unrealistic pace we have set, instead of recognizing that our approach to achieving the goal didn't take into account any of our other values or commitments, we give up on the goal entirely. Even worse, we often feel like we aren't capable or like something is wrong with us that we can't achieve the goal. This is simply not true. The problem isn't that we aren't capable. The problem is that we set a goal without a boundary. And all relationships without boundaries are destined for struggle.

Expect and Celebrate Resistance

Finally, please be prepared for pushback when you set any kind of new boundary, whether that be with goal-setting, within the context of your daily schedule, or in relationships. When you protect your own priorities, those who benefit most from your constant availability are bound to be upset. Unrealistic expectations about how people will respond to new boundaries often cause people to give up quickly or to cave to normal pushback upon setting the boundaries.

On her podcast, *We Can Do Hard Things*, bestselling author Glennon Doyle explains that setting boundaries happens in two parts. First, you have the conversation where you set the boundary. You say it. You tell someone how you would like to be treated, how you will no longer be treated, or that you will no longer be available to them in a way that you may have been in the past. Or, as we covered in this chapter, you implement a new habit like releasing your attachment to the outcomes of those you lead or you take action on something more concrete, like adding the Six Most Important Things List to your daily routine. Most people mistakenly think *this* is the hardest part, but it is not.

The hard part is the second step in the process. This is when you get to experience and deal with the blowback from setting the new boundary. Doyle describes this part as being like a newly planted little tree. You stick your baby roots down in the ground as far as you can, and then you hold on for dear life to face the storm that follows. The storm is the emotional response of those who are affected by the boundary. This can look like a screaming tantrum for the child who is no longer allowed to sleep in a parent's bedroom, the silent treatment from a mother-in-law who is no longer allowed to interrupt your family's plans, or being the subject of cruel-spirited gossip from an employee who isn't behaving appropriately and who has been called out for her unacceptable behavior in her performance review. This can also be an "urgent" text from someone you lead who wants to dump on you while you are at your son's baseball game, or an email that distracts you from an item on your Six Most Important Things List that might generate a new client.

For whatever reason, the storm typically hits us in the area of our lives where we feel *most* vulnerable. If my deepest fear is being alone, it comes in the form of having no one to sit with at an upcoming event. If I secretly feel unsure that I am a good mom, it can mean a teenager screaming, "I hate you! You're the worst mom in the entire world!" at the top of her lungs. If I am worried about losing employees in a tight labor market, it can mean having a worker with a specific area of expertise threaten to leave.

The hardest part of setting a boundary is dealing with the strong feedback we receive in response to our changes. Most of us feel horrible when we receive this feedback, or we interpret a person's negative reaction to our choices as a sign that we did something wrong rather than a confirmation of our progress. If we expect this as a normal part of the process of change, we are much more likely to persist with the better habit moving forward. No one said this kind of change is easy, but most agree that it is absolutely worth it. And guess what? If the boundary you set was too hard or you didn't communicate it well (since you're new to this and won't do it perfectly), you can reset it, change it, adjust it. But strong pushback is not the sign that the boundary needs changing; your healed intuition will guide you to that next move.

CHAPTER 7 EXERCISE
PROTECT YOUR TIME AND ENERGY

Here are some small first steps you can take if it is time to set new boundaries in your work and life.

- Practice the "ribbon cutting" exercise after a difficult conversation with someone you lead, reminding yourself after the meeting that "what's mine is mine, and what's yours is yours."

- In your journal, write down the parts of your life that need to be considered when setting goals. What caregiving responsibilities have you taken on in your life? Does your partner have a demanding career that requires you to be more flexible? Do you have any limitations on your energy, maybe because of health issues or commitments to volunteer roles?

- Then write down one or two goals that *include* boundaries, ensuring you are considering all parts of your life in your pursuit of what you want.

- Also, as you start to set new boundaries, jot down where you anticipate getting resistance to these new relational guidelines. From where will the strongest resistance come? Keep in mind that for most of my clients, the resistance is actually far less than what they anticipate! Sometimes they get none at all! It's simply important to pay attention to resistance when you've set a new boundary and to see it as proof that you are making progress.

8

Money Is a Mirror

AN I ask you to pause for a moment and think about your money? How much money do you have? With whom do you share your money or to what important causes do you give it? How do you exchange your money for goods and services you need on a daily basis? What do you do to earn money? Does money move freely around you, or does it feel stuck and stagnant? And where is all of your money? Take a moment and peruse in your mind all the places where you keep it: your checking account, your investment portfolio, your savings account, and maybe even the cash that is in your wallet right now. Most importantly, when you do a quick, impromptu mental scan of your money, what are your first, most raw, unfiltered thoughts and feelings?

Are you nervous that there isn't enough? Overwhelmed by what to do with what you have? Out of touch with what is there or isn't? In denial about how much you owe and to whom you owe it? Excited about the growth of your investments? Fearful that you aren't adequately prepared for the future? Full of shame about past choices you have made? Proud of some new systems you have put in place to manage it? Embarrassed that what is there isn't what everyone else might think is there? Do you feel safe or like you are teetering on the edge of complete failure? Maybe you feel peaceful and abundantly secure?

Now that you've quickly identified the first, most uninhibited thoughts and feelings you have when you think of your money, I want to introduce a significant and sometimes painful truth: *Your relationship with money is a powerful mirror of your relationship with yourself.* Everything that just came to the surface in this brief scan of your finances has something important to tell you if you will simply pay attention. Money is a powerful mirror.

We all interact with money in some way on a daily basis, and just as we have relationships with people with whom we interact on a daily basis, we all have a relationship with money. If we let it, this relationship can teach us so much about ourselves. Most importantly, the feelings that come up when we think of our money reveal the truest feelings we have about ourselves. Your finances aren't really what caused the fear, insecurity, or any of the feelings that may have come up when you did this brief exploration. Your relationship with your money is just reflecting those feelings that you have about yourself back to you.

Let me give you a personal example. I recently wrote these words about our money in the margin of one of my all-time favorite books, *The Illusion of Money* by Kyle Cease: "I feel a little out over my skis and deeply uncomfortable at this moment as we work to sell our house and to buy the new one... our dream house. It is magnificent... and expansive... and opulent. Wow. This whole buying process brings up some old thought habits, I think, some fears of not enough, not being worthy, feeling like this new house is too much for me. Like I haven't really earned it yet. Maybe I don't know *for sure* if I do deserve to live in a place like this one. Can we actually afford it? I think so. All the numbers say yes, but what if we really can't?"

Sure, I was nervous when I wrote this little quip about the complicated financial logistics of buying a new home. Would our offer on the new house be accepted? Would our old house sell in time to make this transaction happen? Would all the financing go through without a hitch? Those were all concrete potential obstacles in the process. But *really* my nerves had little to do with these financial hurdles and more to do with my deepest feelings about myself. Can you see how those words were truly more about *me*? Was I worthy of living in a house like the one we were buying? Did I really deserve to have this dream come true? Again, money can show us a lot if we pay attention.

The path I have traveled from underearning to believing I do deserve our dream home and so much more over the last five years has been more about changing my habits of thinking than it has been about money. A transformation happened inside of me first, and it was reflected in my relationship with money. The amount of money in our bank accounts grew in proportion to my internal growth. Years of overworking and underearning had taken a toll on my self-esteem, teaching me that my value was dependent on how much I could produce or inspire others to produce. I allowed a compensation plan over which I had no control determine what I would get paid for too many years, and I didn't realize how much my contributions were worth in the larger marketplace, so I undervalued them. I frequently questioned whether I was worthy of more influence, impact, and income. This was reflected in my feelings about money.

Had I truly worked hard enough to deserve more money? Who would pay me more than what I was already earning? Were my unique skills and gifts that valuable? Was it possible that I could work less and ask to be paid more for my work? Was I worthy of being paid more? Was I the kind of person who earned *that* much money? Or was that too much for me? Questions like these swirled in my head constantly as I slowly healed.

For a long time, it felt uncomfortable to acknowledge that I do in fact have a unique skillset that is exceptionally valuable in the marketplace. I provide a service that changes people's lives significantly, and I deserve to be paid well for it. Guess what else I have learned to own at a very deep level? *I* am rare and worthy of abundant compensation... simply because I am. (Deep breath—I still have to let the depth of that statement sink in to fully believe it.) In no way do I need to hide from this truth or feel ashamed of asking for what I am worth. Growing my income has been more about healing my self-esteem and understanding my value than it has been about learning a new skill or working more hours. None of the growth of my income was actually about the money. The money has simply been a mirror, a concrete reflection of this kind of deeper growth happening inside of me.

Money and Security

Furthermore, in *The Illusion of Money*, Kyle Cease examines one of the most common unconscious beliefs we hold about money, and it's a belief that has limited my earnings for years. This is the belief that "money equals security." For years, I believed that if I just had enough money, *then* I would finally feel fully safe and secure. The problem was that no matter how much money I made, the same fears of running out or not having enough still haunted me. The truth is that money has nothing to do with our feelings of security unless we let it. We can give money the power to make us feel secure, but that is just us giving our power away to something that can't give us what we are seeking anyway!

Was there a part of you just now that said, "Yeah, that's easy for you to say when you have more than enough money. You haven't seen my credit card statements or my checking account. I've got bills piling up and not enough money to cover them. I am most definitely *not* financially safe or secure, and having more money would sure help."

Your financial reality may be a mess—that's true. But as Cease writes, "Seeing money as your only source of security is also what is cutting you off from the infinite, creative, amazing, inventive being that you are—which would probably make paying rent a lot easier. When we believe money is our security, we create a massive amount of stress around it. In our attempt to create a sense of safety and security through money, we're actually creating fear within ourselves that is blocking our ability to allow new possibilities to show up." When we attach our feelings of safety and security to our financial circumstances, we limit or obstruct our ability to create more money. We become victims of our finances instead of creators of wealth and abundance.

If I have learned anything from living through a global pandemic, it's that we aren't ever fully safe or secure externally. The most unexpected changes can happen overnight in our world that we cannot control and that threaten our finances.

What gives us security is not money; it's connecting with the piece of ourselves that cannot be shaken no matter what happens around us. True security is knowing that we are not victims to our external circumstances. True security is found in being fully present, opening ourselves up to the opportunities and challenges that show up and living in a state of creative energy. We can always choose to create something new with what is right in front of us, no matter what our bank accounts currently look like.

I want to be clear that this doesn't mean living in a fantasy world, believing money is going to start flying at you out of the sky just because you no longer feel afraid. There is real action required to generate income. However, it does mean you are no longer going to accept the idea that your safety and security are *attached* to money. If you feel safe and secure *first*, then and only then will you go out into the world and take active steps to create money, and I guarantee if you are operating in this kind of abundant energy, your efforts will be rewarded richly.

Again, your relationship with money is an accurate mirror of your relationship with yourself. Do you trust yourself? Do you believe yourself to be worthy of abundance? Is your acceptance of yourself conditional and without attachment to your performance or accolades?

You are safe. You are secure. Separate those feelings from your bank account, and you'll see the flow of money start to head in your direction. Even better, this change of direction often happens very quickly.

Get on the Beach

So where should you begin this journey of transformation if you are ready to see a different reflection in the mirror of money? I would start by repositioning yourself in your relationship with it. When fearful thought habits ruled my life, my finances felt like the ocean, and I was in the water, surrounded by cresting waves. When money was plentiful, I would ride the wave of abundance, confident and happy, feeling safe and secure. However, whenever my income dropped, either because of the changes in the economy or a decline in revenue in my business, I would emotionally crash into the

Your relationship with money is a powerful mirror of your relationship with yourself.

ocean with the wave, panicked and embarrassed, often coming up sputtering and soaking wet.

My feeling of safety and my confidence were deeply affected by how much money I was making, the balance of my liquid savings account, and whether we had enough to pay all the bills with some left over or were just scraping by and making ends meet. Because we lived on a variable commission-based income, this was an especially dangerous space from which to operate. Every day, I gave my power away to money, allowing it to impact my feelings of value and worth positively or negatively. It was exhausting.

One of the quotes that has changed my perspective most profoundly over the past five years of personal financial transformation comes from Jen Sincero's book *You Are a Badass at Making Money*. She writes, "Money is a renewable resource. It comes and goes, it ebbs and flows, it's meant to move. When we're cheap about spending it or weird about receiving it, we block its natural course, we put ourselves in a place of lack instead of abundance and our energy becomes 'richus interruptus.'"

This quote resonates so deeply within me because it reminds me daily that money is *supposed* to behave like the ocean. It is supposed to move. There are waves that go up and down. There are tides that go in and out with the seasons. There are times when the water is calmer and others when it is tumultuous and stormy. One thing is certain about the ocean, just like one thing is certain about money—thinking we can totally control either of them is ridiculous. Also, connecting our feelings of safety and security and self-worth to the waves of the ocean is not wise, just as it is not wise to attach them to the highs and lows of our financial lives.

It's our *attachment* to the ebb and flow of money in our lives that steals our best energy, and it takes the precious energy we need to be able to create more income. It's our fear of not having enough or going broke that robs us of the creative, abundant energy that generates wealth. I had to create some distance between my feelings and money in order to get a different result. I had to stop giving it the power to affect how I felt about myself.

Now, let's talk about what my thought habits look like as I think about my finances today. On most days (I'm definitely still a work in progress on this), rather than swimming *in* the ocean like I used to, where I felt every rise and fall so deeply, I conceptually go to the store and buy myself one of those low beach chairs and an umbrella. I walk out of the ocean, dry myself off, and set my chair and umbrella up on the beach. From the beach, I can watch the expected waves of money without allowing it to take me on an emotional ride, robbing me of full presence in my life. The flow of money in and out of my life is separate from my safety and security.

In addition, it's easier to remember that just as there is no lack of water in the ocean, there is no lack of money in the world, so I don't need to be fearful. There is more money all around us than anyone could ever use or imagine. Even more importantly, my value is not affected by the whims of money. I am valuable no matter what happens with my finances.

Let me give you an example of what this beach analogy looks like when it plays out in a real-life experience. My accountant called me in the middle of September to let me know that I had not been setting aside nearly enough money for taxes for one of my businesses for the fiscal year. To my dismay, in addition to the monthly withdrawals that come out for taxes, an additional $30,000 would need to come out of my checking account over the next few months.

Sidebar—I am *fully* aware that $30,000 is more than the annual income of most people in the world. It represents half of what my annual take-home income was not very long ago, and considerably more than I earned as a high school teacher years ago. I also recognize that paying higher taxes only happens when you are earning more. I like to call these "good problems."

Let's start with what I would have done in the past upon receiving this kind of news when I was living in the ocean with my money. I can feel my heart race in my chest now, even just imagining it. I would have been gripped by sheer panic and shame. My thoughts would have started spiraling immediately. "How am I going to come up with an extra $7,000 a month for the next four months? See, *every* time my income grows, I get *punished* and don't even get to keep the money. What is wrong with me that I didn't know that I should've been setting more aside? I should've known better."

I would've spent hours and perhaps even days being scared to death that we wouldn't have enough money to cover this extra withdrawal. Even worse, I would have instantly shifted into frantic overworking mode, adding hours, doing anything I could think of to create more income, taking on projects that do not pay me what I am worth. All my choices and actions would have been driven by fear until I created the income I needed to cover these taxes. Time and time again, caught in this pattern, I would become so exhausted from my frantic pace over a prolonged period of overworking, I would eventually collapse with fatigue or sickness.

I spent *years* living in this cycle. I chased money from a space of fear so often it became one of my strengths. I was a master at figuring out how to come up with money quickly to cover things at the end of the month. I'd sell a bunch of products, I'd creatively move money from one account to another to cover an unexpected bill, or I'd run a last-minute promotion that would increase my commission for the month. But this kind of work, driven by the energy of survival and not abundance, kept my income smaller than it could and should have been.

I am *beyond* proud to tell you what happened instead when I got this call from my accountant. I slowed down and took some deep breaths. I observed myself wanting to shift to my usual frantic, panic mode, and I reminded myself that I was safe no matter what happened with the taxes. My security was not threatened by this experience. I would not give taxes that kind of power over me. I hung up the phone with my accountant and called my assistant who does the bookkeeping to explain to her how much money we owed.

I said to her, "I am choosing to walk through this challenge differently. Most importantly, I want to remember that this challenge is a *good* thing because it means my income is continuing to rise. Let's look at the numbers together and figure out where we can adjust the budget for the next four months to cover this amount. I am going to stay focused on doing the small things every day that *create* income, and I am going to stay calm and peaceful and trust that we will be fine. This is a normal part of running a business. I will not let it throw me for a loop or affect the boundaries I have set between my work and life. I am choosing to walk this road peacefully and stay focused on the larger goal of serving people and growing my business. The money will come if I do that. Money moves toward peace and gratitude."

Partially, I was telling her how we were going to handle it, and partially, I was telling myself.

I *chose* this time to stay on the beach and to continue to work from a space of confidence, focusing on the small daily action steps that create income. I did not give my power away to the situation and jump back into the ocean.

Incredibly, not even two months later, on the first day of November, there was plenty of money in the tax account to

We allow
money to make
us feel unsafe.

cover all the extra payments—all $30,000 of it. Even better, I didn't work twelve-hour days. I didn't accept work that paid me less than I am worth. The money flowed toward me as I continued to focus on serving people and working in my areas of genius. It was unreal. Even my assistant said at the end of it all, "I can't believe you really did that without any stress. You really did just stay focused on your daily steps, and you didn't shift."

Here are a few additional thoughts about this analogy specific to finances and the way we think about money. First, it is much harder to stay out of the water and on the beach with your money when you own your own business or when you work on commission and your income changes month to month. Having a steady paycheck that you get from someone else that isn't impacted by revenue or sales can hide these deeply entrenched thought habits. If you transition from a traditional job to one where your income fluctuates, don't be surprised if these thought habits pop up even if you've never encountered them before.

Remember that not getting a paycheck from someone else tends to *reveal* all these buried thought habits. They were there all along, and I always tell clients that if you want to know every unhelpful thought habit in your brain, leave a traditional workspace and depend on money from a business you own or where you work strictly on commission. This is where you *really* get to discover where you get your feelings of safety and security. I don't recommend you jump into full-time entrepreneurship quickly or without awareness of this phenomenon for that very reason. If you aren't ready, it can *paralyze* you and create all sorts of financial stress.

For most people, separating feelings of safety and security from their finances is *not* their first, habitual response.

You have to deliberately choose to react a different way, and intentionally choosing a new response takes concentrated daily effort.

Next, you cannot get on the beach without really understanding your personal money story and what created your attachment of money to your self-worth in the first place. Each step of my own financial growth has been preceded by some deep rooting out of stories I had created about money. Here are just a few of the stories I had to unearth and replace with less limiting versions:

- "I can't go to the next level in earnings *and* be the kind of mom and wife I want to be. My family will suffer if I become too successful or if the business gets too big."

- "It's selfish to want more. I'm earning enough to pay our bills. I should be satisfied with survival."

- "Someone else, preferably my husband, should take responsibility for this area of my life. If he could or would increase his income, *that* would be the difference-maker. I shouldn't have to be the one to increase what we are earning."

- "To earn more, I will need to work more hours. I'm already maxed out! How can I possibly *do* more?"

Once I identified these subconscious stories and called into question their validity, I was able to write new ones that would serve me better moving forward. After all, as I noted in Chapter 7, if you're going to make up a story, you might as well make up a good one! My family would *not* suffer if I earned more money; they would benefit. I did not have to work more hours to earn more income; I could work fewer hours and earn more! It was *not* selfish to want more, and I did *not* have to wait for anyone else to increase our income.

I could earn more, and I did! What an empowering experience this transformation has been!

Claim a Permanent Space on the Beach

For several years, I've shared my beach analogy with so many of my clients and almost every person, after I explain it, has asked the same question: *How do I get* on *the beach?* I have a few suggestions that can help:

1 Increase your awareness as you interact with money.

2 Watch your pace.

3 Limit your exposure to triggers.

4 Be crystal clear on the behaviors that create the income you want and track them.

5 Hire someone to help you identify and change your thought habits.

Let's take a look at each of these tactics in depth.

1 **Increase your awareness as you interact with money**
Recognize that you are "in the ocean" consumed by your financial circumstances—elated, riding the waves of abundance, or sputtering and fighting for air—and do this without judgment or attachment. Here are some examples of what someone might observe as she watches her own thoughts around money more closely and compassionately:

- "How fascinating that I am panicking about this unexpected expense and my body is responding as if my very life is threatened."

- "I wonder why fear of looking stupid in front of that particular person caused me to shrink within myself and not ask questions until I understood what he was talking about so I could figure out how to finance this important business project."

- "Huh. Interesting that when I am feeling fear about money, I procrastinate on taking the steps toward completing the tasks on my list that would generate new clients, even when I know they are most important to creating income. I am consistently avoiding those small steps... I wonder what's going on here."

Can you hear the neutral tone of these questions and observations? They are full of curiosity, not condemnation and judgment. They don't deny emotion, but they also shift the brain to a more logical thought process. They simply observe from a distance and ask the question, What is *really* going on here? I can vouch from daily use of this technique that this critical pause during which you choose a different habit of thinking is life-changing.

2 Watch your pace

Next, when we are working and living at a very fast pace, it is difficult to shift our thought habits because we aren't aware enough to even recognize them. I find that I'm most at risk of falling into old thought habits that don't serve me when I am one or more of five things: tired, sick, stressed, hungry, or hormonal. While I can't fully control my hormones (though I am completely open to anything and everything that can help as I age), I know that I tend to get tired, sick, stressed, and hungry most when my pace is too fast. I can actually travel further at a slower pace because I am not sliding into thought habits that hinder my progress. Slow down. Pay attention.

Live and work at a pace that allows you to change and grow even when this feels uncomfortable and new.

3 **Limit your exposure to triggers**

One of the disciplines I chose when I was changing some of my thought habits about money was to limit my exposure. I checked my online accounts and checkbook register at most once a day or every couple of days. Even then, I made sure I looked at these numbers during times of the day when I had the best energy so I could be intentional with my responses to the data I encountered. Ten o'clock at night, after a long day of work and family commitments, is *not* the time for me to think strategically about finances. Even now, I look at this data once a day when I am the freshest—in the morning. Before opening my computer, I breathe, ground myself in feelings of safety and security *separate* from what is on that screen, and then I dig into the numbers and make grounded, secure decisions from that energy, not from feelings of fear or lack.

4 **Be crystal clear on the behaviors that create the income you want and track them**

Because I own my own businesses and am responsible for generating my income, the amount of money that is in my bank account today usually reflects the work I did six to nine months ago. Staring at the current numbers that represent my finances does me little good today, particularly if the result of this analysis is that I feel less confident or scared, I don't generate inspired ideas, bring my most powerful energy, or show up for my clients at my best when I'm in that state of mind.

If the amount of money in my account lags behind the work that creates the income, then I've got to be crystal clear on the actions or behaviors that *create* the income. I have learned to celebrate my commitment to and completion of the behaviors and small steps over which I have control more than I celebrate the results.

As counterintuitive as it seems, I try to *not* celebrate the new clients, the number of courses sold, or the income I have earned. Instead, I celebrate my commitment to and completion of the small daily steps I can control because when I focus on those, the results tend to take care of themselves.

Here are a few questions I use to keep myself on track and identify these small daily steps: What action steps are completely in my control that will create the results I want? Which of these action steps can I take today? Am I tracking these small steps and being accountable to them, or am I just fixated on the results?

No matter what is happening in the economy or the world, over twenty years of owning my own business has taught me to fiercely focus on the daily actions that create change and to release my attachment to the results.

5   Hire someone to help you identify and change your thought habits

When I hired my first business coach, I was terrified to pay what felt like a huge amount of money for a personal development experience. Money was exceptionally tight, and there was no guarantee of a financial return on my investment. Not long into the engagement, I realized how little awareness I had of my own subconscious thought habits and how this lack of awareness was negatively impacting my income. I had some significant blind spots that were inhibiting the growth of my business.

As we worked together, my coach helped me recognize how these thought habits were impacting not only my income but my enjoyment of the process of growing my business every day as well. The more I worked on my habits of thinking, the more my income grew, and the investment I

Accountable relationships with other people provide the context for significant, lasting life-change.

made in this coaching feels like pennies now when I think of how much money it has helped me earn over the last decade.

Significant, lasting life-change happens within the context of accountable relationships. A neutral coach who isn't attached to your business outcomes is one of the most important investments you can make in changing your relationship with money. While it can feel selfish to spend this money on your own development, most of my clients attest that it ends up earning them more money than any other investment they've ever made. I can certainly vouch for this myself!

Mostly, I want you to know that it *is* possible to get out of the ocean and up onto the beach even if you've been drowning in the waves for your entire life. I've coached many people through this process and seeing them conquer their limiting beliefs around money is one of the most gratifying parts of my work. Don't lose hope; change is always possible.

We Earn What We Believe We Are Worth

Next, I'd like to share an interesting phenomenon I have observed over two decades of work with women who are growing their own businesses or who earn an income based on their performance and what they produce. So many women will work diligently for a period of time, maybe a few months or even a few years, and they will generate a higher level of income than they have ever had before through their focused efforts. At some point, earning more than they *really* think they are worth creates a subconscious panic that says, "This feels different and uncomfortable, and this could be dangerous." Even though they may *logically* know more income is a positive change, if the level of earning outpaces their feelings of self-worth, it can wreak havoc.

Women who increase their income too quickly or without the personal growth to accompany it will subtly sabotage their own progress and return to a level of income that feels more in alignment with what they *really* feel they are worth. I've seen women get sick, sidetrack themselves with family issues, create conflict with business peers, live in a constant state of disorganization, or stop taking the daily steps that create growth because the growth of their income outpaced their personal growth. Self-sabotage is a sneaky, subtle, subconscious response.

Notably, women who leave traditional jobs to go full-time in more entrepreneurial roles will work to create just about the same level of income they earned in the traditional job they just left. They justify their lack of increased earnings by focusing on the good things that entrepreneurship has brought into their lives: friendship, recognition, community, freedom, and flexibility. However, they can only earn the level of income their subconscious mind believes they are worth even though they are operating in a space that has no earning limits. In the end, we all earn what we really believe we are worth.

If this experience resonates with you, I want to assure you that personal growth almost always precedes professional growth. Until you do the inner work of healing your self-esteem and expanding what you believe you are worth, your income may increase temporarily after a season of intense efforts, but it won't stay there for long. Your subconscious thought habits will make sure you earn only what you *truly* believe you are worth.

Finally, I want to warn you that deep, well-worn patterns of thinking that no longer serve you will continue to reveal themselves as you work to grow your impact, influence, and income. Sometimes these hidden habits are revealed when you least expect it! This happened to me recently on a chilly summer night in the mountains of Utah, as I sat around a fire with some friends who are also business coaches. We had gathered for a few days to sharpen our coaching skills at a weekend retreat. One of the finest people I have met at events like these is my friend Lane Monson.

Lane is an accomplished leader who started his career in sales at IBM and moved his way up the corporate ranks, eventually leading several successful companies as global senior vice president, COO, and eventually CEO. He is kind and gracious, and when I am in his space and talking with him, it feels like I am physically enveloped in a bubble filled with his pure, unfaltering belief in me.

On this night, Lane and I were hashing over what we had learned during the day's sessions, and during the conversation, I offhandedly asked him, "Do you have a financial goal for your business this year? Like, what do you want to earn?"

Without hesitation, he said, "I do. My goal is to earn $750,000 this year."

Shit.

I don't swear. And when I do, I usually don't do it well. But the instant Lane said "$750,000," this is the *only* word that popped into my head, and it was EM-PHAT-IC!

Shit! Shit! SHIT!

You see, since our life-changing meeting with our financial advisor I had made *so much* progress in overcoming my years of underearning. I had more than doubled my income, and I had done it working fewer hours and doing work that was fulfilling and deeply impactful. And yet my own income goal for the year was $300,000, and until this moment, that felt attainable but lofty and extravagant, maybe even a bit much if I must confess. In one sentence, and without even meaning to, Lane had caught me *still* undervaluing myself.

Lane is outstanding. Don't get me wrong. He's one of the coolest, most accomplished people I know. He elevates people with his coaching, has an impressive trove of experiences that serve his clients, and he is wicked smart. He *deserves* a $750,000 reward for his contributions.

But guess what? So am I, and so do I.

SHIT.

It was glaringly obvious to me at that moment that what separates the two of us is only one thing—*what we believe we are worth*. While I am learning my value, I'm still not *fully* owning it.

When I asked Lane about our conversation later, he said, "It never crossed my mind as I moved up the ranks and earned more in corporate America that I didn't deserve it. At each step, I felt like I was being compensated at my level of contribution. I knew I was making an impact on the team and the success of the business that warranted that kind of compensation. I feel the same now. The more I contribute, the more I expect to be compensated."

There it is. There is the thought habit that I am still wrestling with every day, and I realize it's probably left behind residue from years of being vastly underpaid for my significant professional contributions. Lane, on the other hand, has a beautiful blend of expectation and understanding. Expecting to be compensated, and understanding the value of your contribution. It's not about working harder or longer. It's about standing unwaveringly in your intrinsic value.

My wish for you is that your life is full of Lanes, people whose very *being* forces you to look into the mirror of your money honestly and to own your value. When confronted with their humble excellence, may what you see inspire you to step into a new level of abundance without hesitation or apology.

CHAPTER 8 EXERCISE
YOUR MONEY MIRROR

Hold your "money mirror" up to yourself and see what you discover by answering these questions in your journal:

- Describe your financial situation right now. How would you describe your relationship with money?

- What are the immediate and strongest feelings that come up when you think about your money?

- If, as I wrote in this chapter, "Your relationship with money is a powerful mirror of your relationship with yourself," what is your money saying to you right now?

9

Do a Thorough Check
of Your Environment

As a woman who has worked for over two decades to help other women grow and develop, I'd like to offer an observation that is rarely spoken about but affects all of us. Many women exhale audibly with relief, feeling deeply affirmed and validated when I explain this idea to them, because while they have lived its truth for their entire professional lives, having someone say it out loud and acknowledge it feels so good.

Here it is: women are currently living and working within many invisible but powerful systems that were not created with their best interests in mind. The spaces in which we work and parent and serve were not made for or by us. This isn't to say these systems are all bad or harmful to everyone; in fact, for a shrinking number of people who have thrived socially and financially within these systems, they work exceptionally well. I do think, however, that we must all acknowledge that most of our current social and economic systems were created for a world that no longer exists.

Let me explain this a bit more concretely. The systems that still provide the framework of our collective life experiences today were built for a world in which men would leave their homes to go to work for a set period of time each day, leaving their wives at home to take care of children, the house, and all of the things related to their families. Since the 1960s, women have tried to do the work that only men used to do outside of the home while *also* continuing to do all of the other work in the home at the same time.

While our efforts have been valiant and we have made considerable progress professionally, our attempts to succeed within this system in dual roles have largely resulted in lackluster incomes, exhaustion, and burnout. We often end up misinterpreting our slow, hindered progress or our lack of progress altogether as the result of some deficiency on our part. Rather than seeing this struggle as a symptom of operating within an outdated, poorly functioning system, the experience can feel like a repeated and unfair sucker punch to our confidence and self-esteem. Exhausted from ramming into these unsupportive structures time and time again, we repeatedly ask questions like, "What's wrong with me that I can't build the size of business I want to build or be promoted to that next position? If I am capable of that next level of income or influence, why can't I figure it out? Is there a secret formula or skillset that I am missing?"

Can I abruptly and enthusiastically disrupt this destructive, damaging chain of questions to ask you an important question: *Is the system in which you are operating even capable of creating what you want?*

I was talking with one of my clients whom I'll call Sarah, and she shared several powerful examples of how the systems that support men working and women staying home haven't changed, even as that reality has. After her second child,

Sarah and her husband decided that following her maternity leave, he would stay home to take care of the household and their two young children so she could focus on her corporate career. However, even having him home full-time didn't fully relieve Sarah of the burden of caring for her family—at least not the way it did for her male peers.

She described those years saying, "It's like an axe straight down your center. There's a piece of you that wants to succeed in your career, but you also want to be a successful parent. The system isn't set up for women to succeed in both arenas without sacrificing themselves almost completely. That's not fair. You're serving those two worlds and driven to be the best in both. Eventually, the person in the middle trying to hold up both is going to crack."

One year on her daughter's birthday, she was out of town at an intense meeting with her very demanding boss. When she told her boss that she needed to wrap up the conversation that had gone way past normal business hours so she could catch the last flight home that night on her daughter's special day, her boss told her that was just unacceptable. Though it was uncomfortable and not well received, Sarah replied, "I'm leaving. It's my daughter's birthday, and I at least want to kiss her good night." She has no doubt that interactions like these slowed her progress up the corporate ranks and kept her from being able to freely pursue opportunities her male counterparts did. She was every bit as intelligent and skilled, but the system didn't allow her to be both the kind of mom and business professional she wanted to be.

Sarah also told me that out of town meetings were often scheduled on Halloween or Valentine's Day. While neither are major holidays for those without children, those were important moments that Sarah didn't want to miss with her kids. She would stay up late preparing thoughtful Valentine's gifts for her husband to leave out, or she would have to use vacation time to be there for trick-or-treating. Watching her juggling being a mom with her demanding work schedule, people would often say to her, "I don't know how you do it all." She says she always replied, "I don't know any different. I just do it."

Probably the most poignant example she shared of the challenges of working in the traditional world was an annual event hosted by the Radiological Society of North America that has been held in Chicago for over one hundred years. Every year, radiologists gather with their colleagues the week after Thanksgiving to network, learn from each other, and share professional development resources. Marketing people, support staff, and vendors like Sarah whose companies want to work with these doctors have to give up their entire Thanksgiving weekend every year to set up for the conference. Here's the kicker: Sarah learned from some people who had been a part of the event for decades that the *only* reason the event is held at this inconvenient time of year is because the radiologists all used to bring their wives with them so they could do their Christmas shopping on the Magnificent Mile while their husbands were at the conference. Even though the world has changed and many spouses of the doctors now have their own careers, women *are* the doctors, or not all doctors celebrate Christmas, the structure of the event continues to support a way of life that, for most, no longer exists.

As I navigate being a working mom, I *constantly* encounter systems that are set up for families who have one parent home and one working. Preschool hours are practically impossible for working parents, two or three hours placed smack-dab in the middle of the workday. Constant early dismissals and days off school for holidays and professional development for teachers are extremely challenging. Many athletic events start at four o'clock or happen on long weekends that include Fridays. Don't even get me started on summers! Summer sports and music camps offered by schools often happen throughout the day all week long. There are few if any quality, affordable options available for childcare, especially for kids old enough to not need constant attention but who still need something other than screens to fill their time. And what happens when someone gets sick or has an orthodontist appointment or a concert or performance that happens during the school day? Interestingly, a friend of mine who is a physician and whose husband has stayed home full-time to raise their children shared that in spite of their reversal of traditional roles, when a child was sick or needed something, the school still always contacted her first.

Our traditional economic system was not created with working women in mind, and it was created for a world that no longer exists.

There are some rays of hope for working women. We are in the midst of a cultural transformation of how we define the concepts of work and business. New definitions of these two concepts are breaking the mold of our traditional views and becoming the new normal, especially as our workforce becomes more diverse. Because I work with people who are operating in both of these versions, I feel like I have a front-row seat to this change.

Traditional Work and Business

Let's start with a look at the traditional definitions of work and business.

Where: In the traditional work world, a person gets up in the morning, gets dressed, leaves the home, takes his or her children to a childcare provider or school, and drives to an office in a "brick and mortar" building.

Communication Tools: To communicate, he or she uses a landline phone to call and talk to people. Email is another main source of communication with clients, peers, and leaders. These places of work still use paper mail delivered through the post office as a common form of communication.

Networking: If someone in a traditional work setting wants to network and meet new people, he or she will leave the office after normal work hours to attend golf outings, rotary club meetings, chamber events, or perhaps serve on a board of some sort in the local community.

Marketing: These types of businesses use radio or TV for their marketing, along with billboards, newspapers, and paper mail. They also may host booths at events or be sponsors for teams or local organizations in exchange for publicity.

Attire: The dress in a traditional business is more formal, professional attire. Often shirts and ties for men, and dress pants or a skirted suit or dress for women.

Values: These types of environments value education. They want to know what you have a degree or degrees in and where you got them, and often your salary depends on these accomplishments. They value a linear career path where you work to be promoted to the position above you either through your performance or increased education, and more prestigious titles and ranks result in more income.

Hours: Most of these work environments expect you to keep a standard nine-to-five schedule, and promotions almost always bring with them the unspoken expectation that you will add a few hours to your workweek.

Income: As I said earlier but want to reiterate, income in a traditional work world is based on your education, the position and title you have, and sometimes on your years of experience. Performance can also play a role, though not always. Relationships are important in moving up the ranks, and well-connected people are more likely to get promotions and raises.

Social Media Presence: While there may be a perfunctory social media business page that some intern or young staff person is paid to create and keep up-to-date, social media is largely seen as something on the fringe, just another form of communication. Traditional businesses may even hire someone to create and post targeted ads on social media. It's part of the budget, something you have to do "nowadays." The people who work in traditional business models may have social media accounts for personal reasons, and they almost all have LinkedIn accounts for professional reasons, but they view Instagram and Facebook as recreational and superfluous.

Energy: The energy of the work environment is very linear and structured. There are job descriptions, job performance metrics, structures to control time off, and deadlines and goals.

Support Staff: The support staff work in the office assisting those with higher rank and pay. Their primary role is to protect those they support from busywork and interruptions. They are almost always women.

New and Emerging Work and Business

Now, let's look at what work and business look like in this new emerging economy.

Where: In this new world, people work from home, they work in coffee shops, they work *anywhere* that they can find a great internet connection. Most of these businesses do not have a physical location or office space. I actually wrote this entire chapter in a coffee shop in a different state while there for a basketball tournament for my son!

Communication Tools: To communicate, a person in this world relies heavily on text messages, Facebook Messenger, Instagram private messages, and video-meeting platforms like Zoom, FaceTime, or Microsoft Teams. They often also use other communication apps like Slack, Voxer, or Marco Polo for a more holistic virtual communication experience.

Networking: They grow their network mostly through social media, attending family or their kids' events, or occasionally flitting in and out of community or chamber events, and they don't always realize they are networking, nor do they do it out of obligation. Their work is an extension of their daily lives, and as life travels, so does their business. Sometimes, their lives *are* their businesses, as it is for people who are social media influencers and earn income promoting content, products, or experiences to their followers.

Marketing: They market mostly through personal, interactive social media—Facebook or Instagram, most commonly, depending on the demographic they want to attract. For example, one of my clients is a photographer who largely focuses on taking senior year pictures. She is all over Instagram and even has a "mod squad" of about twenty specially

You can love the messenger and leave the message.

selected high school seniors each year. These students post their portraits on their social media accounts, which organically spreads the word about the photography business in exchange for extra pictures and fun group experiences with the mod squad. This new business model rarely pays for any form of traditional advertising.

Attire: The work attire in this new economy is much more casual, especially from the waist down. Some people put on a nice shirt or are all business up top for important meetings on a video-conferencing platform—but many might work out in the morning and then stay in their exercise or comfy clothes until late in the day or even all day. I recently showed up at a traditional business meeting in a board room wearing a trendy athletic jumpsuit with high top sneakers and a knit stocking cap. My friend who is an administrator at our local hospital sat next to me at the table wearing his full navy suit and tie. We had a good chuckle about the image the two of us sitting next to each other created: what a vivid visual representation of the differences between these two worlds!

Values: This new work world values contribution and the size of your sphere of influence. It counts followers, likes, clicks, and views. The value you bring to the marketplace is measured by outcomes, not the evaluation of someone in a position senior to yours. It also places a high value on the freedom and flexibility that create work-life balance, many times even over income.

Hours: If you ask someone who works in this new way what their hours are, they will laugh. Who is counting or knows? They have a flexible schedule around family, childcare availability, and other life priorities. Is this work? Is it not? It's not always clear. Sometimes, they get up early on a Sunday morning to get some work done, and sometimes they work from their cars in between baseball games at the local sports complex.

Income: Earnings in this space are completely based on performance. If you add value to other people, and you have influence with them, your income will grow, and you will serve more people, sell more products, or be able to grow your organization more effectively. Education may provide useful skills, but it certainly isn't a prerequisite for earning more money.

Social Media Presence: As far as social media goes, the people who work in this world don't see platforms like Facebook, Instagram, TikTok, and YouTube as simply recreational or just another tool in the marketing toolbox. These online platforms are truly the vehicle that creates income. They live *through social media*; it is often how they create money. They rarely "log off" their accounts as communication comes through those portals from those they lead, their customers, and their potential customers. They boldly seek more followers, likes, and friends, and they use those connections to grow their networks and businesses very intentionally. They probably post multiple times a day and follow and understand and pay close attention to changes to algorithms so they can get their products or services in front of more people.

Energy: The energy of this work environment is very collaborative, *not* linear. It requires blending personal and business, sharing ideas, and watching what others are doing and learning from it. Life and work are often tangled together. The energy of one is the energy of the other.

Support Staff: Finally, if the people who work in this environment have support staff, it's often virtual. They may have one or more people that come into their homes to work, and they may have multiple virtual assistants who do different jobs for them, operating largely in the same type of work-from-home model. I've never physically been in the presence of my business manager who lives in Boston and has supported me and the growth of my business for years. She has clients all over the country.

Observations and Predictions

While you certainly know which world you operate in, you can also probably name lots of people you know who work in the other world. Some people even work in both. Even though it doesn't now, I believe the traditional work world is eventually going to represent a minority of people. While many might resist this prediction or even vehemently disagree, I am excited about the transition because I believe that this new system of commerce was created with all people in mind, not only men who work outside of the home. My hunch is that most people will eventually work at least part of the time in this new emerging model and type of business. Even if they have a traditional job during the day, more and more people will have a side hustle or do something to supplement their traditionally earned income.

One of the things I noticed during the pandemic is that people who had multiple sources of income were able to navigate the challenges of the crisis much more peacefully. If their traditional job started laying people off or if they had to take a pay cut, they did more of their other work to fill in the gaps. If you only have one source of income for your family and the industry you work in is crippled or, even worse, immobilized by a crisis like a pandemic, the economic stress on you and your family can be extremely high.

While the extreme changes caused by the pandemic were probably once-in-a-generation occurrences, I think the increasing volatility of our economy is here to stay. Being diversified in your work and having multiple streams of income is a wise strategy. The traditional business model won't be erased completely, but I think it will start to look much more like this new definition in the future.

The pandemic certainly increased the pace of this change as people who worked from home found that it was just as effective and a better fit for their lives outside of work too. Businesses in the emerging model have also shown themselves to be better prepared to deal with and adapt to this quickly evolving economy. They tend to be more innovative and adaptable, and because they are already dependent on technology, they didn't have to create any new pathways for business interactions to happen. Some may have slightly shifted their process, marketing, messaging, or some of their products or offerings, but other than that, not a lot changed for them when the world shut down. It was pretty much business as usual.

It's also much more profitable to run a business in the new work model because you don't have the expense of renting or buying a physical location. Locations are becoming more and more virtual. How much virtual "real estate" you own in terms of your website presence or number of followers is now often more important than how much physical real estate you own.

For years, I can remember going to chamber events and being dismissed or brushed off by traditional business leaders who saw my home-based business as a hobby or something I could do to be home with my kids. While I didn't like their snubs, I found solace knowing that the business I ran was much larger and much more profitable than theirs, even though I didn't have a storefront or title that they understood.

All leaders who work in traditional business models would do well to at least think about whether they are connecting with and marketing to those working in the new work world effectively. They are a huge source of influence and of potential revenue, no matter what your business is.

Here are some good questions to ask yourself in this transitional period: Are the people who work in this new, emerging world your customers? Do they know about your products or services? If not, how would they find out about your services or products? Where would they interact with you or your business and how?

Do an overall scan of your client base. What is the demographic? Is it a mix of people who work in both worlds or more heavily one or the other? For example, if you work at a bank, are most of your loans with people in a traditional work world? How would someone who works from home and operates and communicates through social media know about the products your bank offers? Don't get lulled into thinking you "have that social media thing covered" because you have a "business page" where someone makes boring posts once a week, so your audience will find you or see you. You're missing a huge opportunity if you are not visible and accessible to them through their communication networks.

For example, a few months ago, I was doing a workshop with a group of state representatives and realized that I had never once been contacted directly about donating to a politician's campaign. Not once. I've never even personally encountered the representatives from my district. I live and work in this new, different world. If local and state politicians could connect in a meaningful way through social media with people like me, we could be a huge source of donations and, of course, votes. I'm deeply invested in what's happening in our economy. I own two growing businesses. I'm influential in my community, but most government leaders are missing me because I'm not at their traditional places of connection. It's worth the time and effort to consider where you can find me and people like me.

Also, do a general scan of your employees. How diverse is your employee base (culture, race, gender, age, etc.)? How about the upper-level leadership teams? If your business or these influential groups within it lack diversity, could it be because you are operating in a very traditional work environment, one that isn't accessible to women who don't have the built-in advantages the traditional work world requires? Diversity *requires* flexibility.

Many brilliant and talented minorities and women have left the traditional business model to create this new work model because they grew weary of not being able to move forward as quickly as they were capable. Are most promotions in your workplace given to the people who are able to go out for drinks or who play golf together outside of work hours? Are these opportunities available to those who don't have the luxury of recreational connecting points because they have to get home to care for children or aging parents? Or is there a pattern of hiring or promoting people who attended the same schools or who move in the same social circles as the current leaders? Often women have been overlooked for leadership roles that have more influence and financial rewards because the demands of parenting or caretaking didn't allow them to be a part of the after-hours networking that might help them to advance. If you see a lot of people who look the same at your place of work—age, race, gender, culture—the model in which you operate could be a big reason why.

Is working from home a possibility for your employees? Do you have the technology infrastructure to make that happen? Can you invest money to make it a possibility—both for the immediate situation but also for the future employee who wants a more flexible work-life experience? What new

The thought habits that stand in your way will almost certainly come up to get your attention when you decide to offload unpaid labor.

communication tools and systems need to be in place to even make this an option for really great employees? Especially if you are having trouble finding or retaining great talent, could some changes toward the new work world be needed?

Let's also take some time to run the experience of working at your business through the filter of people with children: Is it an appealing place of work for young, bright, creative people who have small children? Does your way of working allow for them to parent the way they want to? Can they get their kids on the bus in the morning and be home to see them off the bus too? Are networking opportunities within your organizations offered at times that are not accessible to parents with school-aged children? Seven o'clock in the morning before school or four to six p.m. are the worst times for parents to attend events, but that's when many social connection points and formal business networking events take place. Are the demands of the higher leadership roles at your company even possible for someone without a spouse or caregiver at home to take care of children and home responsibilities? You're missing out on great leaders and great potential employees for your business if you are too rigid with the way you are running things.

Finally, I'll close by saying that this change may feel very uncomfortable and maybe even threatening to you if the traditional model of work has served you well. I can empathize. Why would you want something that feels safe and predictable to change? You may be tempted to brush this whole idea aside thinking, "Once we're through the pandemic and its aftermath, everything will go back to normal." At the time of writing this book, many have returned to the office, but many have not. I want to nudge you a bit and let you know that even if you didn't notice, normal was already shifting. The normal we knew on March 1, 2020, is never coming back.

Take these questions seriously, and see if you can be more flexible and open. It will serve you well moving forward.

Unpaid Labor

Remember my friend and fellow coach Lane Monson? We had a conversation recently in which we were talking about the unique challenges that women face in the work world. At the very moment in our conversation when a delivery guy pulled into our driveway with the balloons I had ordered for my son's sixteenth birthday, Lane said to me, "In all of my years as I moved up the corporate ranks and when I was a CEO, I never had to think about ordering balloons for the birthday parties or buying or wrapping presents. My wife takes care of all those home and family jobs. My responsibility was simply to go to work and to excel there." I still can't believe he said those words just as the doorbell to my house rang for that balloon delivery—pretty meaningful, and telling timing!

I want to acknowledge this very significant difference in the life and work experiences of men and women. Even though most of us are now working full-time, women continue to do most of the unpaid labor in our world. I'm a master at delegation, and though I don't personally *do* all the work, I am still the one in our house who plans and makes sure that all gifts are bought and wrapped, the Easter eggs are filled with candy, the food is purchased and prepared for family celebrations, and the cake and candles are ready for birthday parties.

I'm not complaining or resentful, and my husband, Ryan, will gladly help with any household chores or task if I ask him, but in the end, when I think about the slow and steady pace at which my businesses have grown over the past two decades, I have to acknowledge that all the work and planning I do for our family takes a great deal of time and energy. Some of it I enjoy, and most of it I want to do, but I don't ever have the luxury of *only* focusing on my work.

If you are a woman, and if at times you feel like your progress is slower or more draining than it is for your male peers, it probably is—so stop feeling bad about it. More importantly, it isn't slower because you aren't as capable; it's because you're carrying a heavier load of unpaid labor outside of work. I see so many leaders who are trying to lead at a high level in their work *and* trying to be a perfect parent *and* trying to run a household *and* trying to nurture a marriage or partnership *and* trying to volunteer in their schools and communities *and* trying to take care of themselves at a high level *and*, maybe even at the same time, trying to grow a fledgling business.

Because of this huge, heavy load of responsibilities, there is always a fair amount of chaos around women, and they almost always feel behind or overwhelmed. Even more often, I see these growing leaders blame *themselves* for a lack of ability to maintain structure or to make progress in their lives when the problem is something much larger. They are trying to do the impossible. They are trying to do well at so many things that are all full-time endeavors; many expect themselves to do it all perfectly, and then they blame themselves when they are unable to do them all. Again I'll ask, *Is the system in which you are operating even capable of creating what you want?*

Let's dig deeper into this concept of unpaid labor. In her book *The Moment of Lift*, Melinda Gates defines unpaid labor as "work performed in the home, like childcare or other forms of caregiving, cooking, cleaning, shopping, and errands, done by a family member who's not getting paid."

Most women don't even quantify the amount of time and energy this work takes on a daily, weekly, and monthly basis. We just do it without thinking.

Gates also makes a poignant point: "The most powerful positions in society are often occupied by men who do have wives who do not work outside the home. And those men may not fully understand the lives of the people who work for them."

When you think of the most powerful positions in your community—at your hospitals, at the largest businesses in the towns where you live, in your highest-ranking government positions—are the most powerful positions mostly held by men? In addition, do most of those men have wives who do not work outside the home? I'd like to challenge you to recognize that the reason so many of those men have had the time and energy to move into those positions is *because* they have someone doing the bulk of the unpaid labor in their lives. They spend no time or energy wondering what they will eat, where they will get the food to eat, whether the clothes they want to wear are clean, or even if they have enough grounds to make their morning cup of coffee!

The Bureau of Labor Statistics provides telling numbers about the current makeup of the workforce in the United States. In 2022, 56.8 percent of all American women worked outside the home, and a whopping 75 percent of women between the ages of twenty-five and fifty-four (the peak ages of parenting and caretaking) did. Based on these statistics, we know that most American women are not *solely* responsible for taking care of children and the home. Clearly, the majority of women are actively engaged in the workplace. However, as women have left the home to work, they have also continued to carry the bulk of the weight of caregiving and homemaking, the unpaid labor in our world.

I'd like you to take a quick survey I created that allows you to assess how many hours per month you do spend on unpaid work. Next to each category of unpaid labor, I want you to estimate the number of hours you spend each *month* doing this kind of work. You can write the same list and fill this out in your journal; add up your total number of hours and then divide by four to come to an *estimate* of how much unpaid labor you are doing each week. Obviously, this varies based on several factors that change during different seasons of the year and life, but we are just looking for an estimate.

Unpaid Labor Survey

Deep Cleaning
Washing and sweeping floors, cleaning bathrooms, dusting, vacuuming, washing windows, etc.

Estimated monthly hours: _____

Kitchen Duty
Loading and unloading dishwasher, washing dishes, wiping down counters, cleaning out the fridge, tidying up after meal prep and after meals, etc.

Estimated monthly hours: _____

Picking Up
Putting away toys, books, mail, clothes, shoes, bags, etc.

Estimated monthly hours: _____

Shopping

Purchasing clothes, shoes, outerwear, and sporting equipment for everyone in your family, ordering or shopping for food, making returns for online shopping, bringing outgrown clothes to the resale shop, etc.

Estimated monthly hours: _____

Outside Work

Mowing, weeding, raking leaves, taking out garbage, washing vehicle, etc.

Estimated monthly hours: _____

Bookkeeping

Paying bills, managing budget, calling about utilities and phones, updating credit card information when cards expire, managing investments, preparing for and filing taxes, moving money to savings, securing insurance, etc.

Estimated monthly hours: _____

Caregiving

Caring for babies or small children and elderly parents or family members, helping kids with homework, days off for sick children, driving kids or elderly relatives to activities or meetings, feeding and caring for pets, etc.

Estimated monthly hours: _____

Food

Planning, preparing, and serving meals or food to take to social gatherings, packing lunches, etc.

Estimated monthly hours: _____

Coordination and Appointments

Haircuts, dentists, doctors, oil changes and other vehicle maintenance, accountants, financial advisors, orthodontists, chiropractors, lessons and practices, carpools, etc.

Estimated monthly hours: _____

Special Occasions

Birthday parties, holiday parties, food prep for these events, buying and wrapping gifts, sending invitations, cleanup after events, thank-you notes.

Estimated monthly hours: _____

Packing and Unpacking

For vacations, day trips, sporting events, family events, etc.

Estimated monthly hours: _____

Laundry

Washing and drying clothes, folding, ironing, handwash and hang dry, dry cleaning, etc.

Estimated monthly hours: _____

Total Estimated Monthly Hours of Unpaid Labor: _____

Estimated Weekly Hours of Unpaid Labor: _____

(Divide total monthly hours by four)

Are you astonished by the final number? Do you now know why you are so tired all the time? Do you understand why you can't figure out how to grow your side hustle into a business that allows you to leave your full-time job? You aren't just working a full-time job that you're getting paid for and trying to build a business on the side; you're also working a full-time job for which you are not getting paid!

According to Gates, "On average, women do seven years more unpaid work than men over their lifetimes. That's about the time it takes to complete a bachelor's *and* a master's degree." One economist, Marilyn Waring, traveled around the world in 1975 studying the vast quantities of unpaid work done by women. Before her research, there were no published studies about this phenomenon. Gates writes, "[Waring] calculated that if you hired workers at the market rate to do all the unpaid work women do, unpaid work would be the biggest sector of the global economy. And yet economists were not counting this as work." This incredibly lopsided distribution of unpaid labor explains why women are often not part of important decision-making conversations in our communities, why we aren't getting promotions or being awarded high-paying opportunities in the workforce. We are too busy doing all or a large majority of the unpaid labor in our homes.

All of this is not in any way subtracting from the importance of caregiving. It's also saying nothing against the value of the unpaid work we are doing. Much of this work is the glue that holds together our communities and our families. I'm also not saying this work doesn't need to be done. Whatever your gender, if the thing in life you love to do more than any other is to take care of people and your home, I encourage you to do that work with all your heart and soul. Caregiving makes life deeply meaningful. It is a vital part of our culture. If you are in a financial situation that allows you to do this free of charge and that is what you want to do, then by all means, do it! But if you are a woman working full-time and so is your partner, and you are doing a disproportionate amount of the unpaid labor, then I have to ask, *Why?*

Why do women willingly take on all these responsibilities *and* work full-time? What is the cost to our health? To our finances? To our children? To our marriages or relationships? Even more importantly, what do we do about this?

I believe the first step is to stop doing *all* of the unpaid labor. We can either divide it more evenly among the members of our family, or we can hire someone to help us. We cannot continue to think that we can do it all and thrive. Most women are just barely surviving under the burden as it is. However, when I pose eliminating some or all of the unpaid labor as a possible solution to my clients, many immediately backpedal. Even the thought of hiring someone to help with this work triggers *all* sorts of internal resistance. This is where our deeply ingrained thought habits really become an obstacle to our progress.

I have repeatedly asked the phenomenal, brilliant women with whom I work, "If you have struggled to hire help in the past or if you have resisted it, why? Why don't you get hired help?"

Here are some of the answers I get:

- "It feels selfish."

- "I can't afford it."

- "It costs too much."

- "I'd rather spend money on something else."

- "I should be able to do it myself."

- "It's so easy. Why would I pay someone to do it?"

- "I'm embarrassed for someone to see my mess." (Also: "I need to clean before I could ever have someone in here, and I don't have time to do that!")
- "I can't find anyone to help me."
- "Letting someone into my home to help makes me feel too vulnerable."
- "I like things done a certain way, and I don't have time to train someone to do it the way I want."
- "I would be embarrassed if people knew I had help, especially my mom or other close family members. They would be so critical."
- "Only *certain kinds of people* have hired help, and I am not one of them."

If asking for or paying for help carries this much internal resistance, it's no wonder we continue to just do the work.

Unloading the Unpaid Labor

So how do we shift this trend? What do we do about it? How do we shift the balance of unpaid labor in our world and lighten our loads so we can increase our influence, impact, and income?

I've got six suggestions for you.

1   Hire someone to do *one* thing off your unpaid labor survey.
2   Be *very* aware of self-sabotage.
3   Watch for naysayers. They will most definitely show up.
4   Don't depend on husbands, wives, partners, or kids.
5   Recognize the value of unpaid labor.
6   Categorize this as a stewardship issue.

There is nothing wrong with you. You simply don't have enough help.

1   **Hire someone**

I'm shocked at how many women have supportive partners, have the income available to pay someone to clean or do laundry or cook, and they *still* won't give it up. At the very least, pay another woman to do the work so she is earning an income! My friend Erica, for example, supports her family financially with the income she earns running a cleaning business. She loves the work, and she has a flexible schedule because of her business. Why would you not want to support another woman's business that allows you to unload some of the unpaid labor you do? Is there anything wrong with paying someone to do this work so that person can also provide for their family? That feels like a win-win exchange to me! By continuing to carry the burden of this work because you think it's selfish to hire help, you are robbing yourself of your precious energy *and* you are robbing someone else of potential income. No matter which way you cut it, it doesn't make sense. Hiring help is the least selfish course of action you could take!

If you are going to choose one thing to eliminate, start with what is most draining to you. If you love to cook, then cook! If you love to iron, then iron! But I know you don't love every single thing you are doing that is on that unpaid labor list. There is something on there that just makes you groan when you think of it, or you're so behind on it all the time that you are constantly feeling the stress of not taking care of it.

Right now, I want you to look at that list and pick one thing. You don't have to get rid of everything at once, but you can get rid of one thing.

2   **Be *very* aware of self-sabotage**

As you look at the list and choose one thing to hand off to someone else, I want you to pay really close attention to what your brain is *screaming* at you. I can almost guarantee that if allowing others to help you is a new choice, it will remind you quite loudly: "You don't have the money for that! Who do you think you are? You can't let someone into your messy home! How embarrassing! My mom 'did it all,' so I should be able to do it all too!"

Don't fight it; just observe the resistance. What is the root of it? Where does it come from? Is it a message you learned about your role as a woman from watching family members? Is this message in alignment with your gifts and values or something you absorbed without evaluating whether it works for you? Even deeper, does doing all this unpaid labor protect you from the influence or income or impact you say you want? Because if you were really that successful, people might notice you? You might be really great? Could that success open you to criticism and critique from others? Maybe you would make more money than what feels comfortable to you if you had more energy, and that terrifies you?

The resistance has something to teach you. It can unearth the stories and subconscious thought habits that are holding you back. It doesn't mean that delegating household tasks to someone else is wrong or bad or that you shouldn't do it. Overcoming this resistance is a normal part of learning to let people help you. The thought habits that stand in your way will almost certainly come up to get your attention when you decide to offload unpaid labor. When you make a huge commitment or a significant decision that will move you in a new, healthy direction, everything inside you that is unlike this brave decision will come up to be healed.

Also, be prepared for your thoughts to become confused. This is one of the most powerful weapons of self-sabotage. You'll think things like, "I wouldn't even know where to start. I don't know who to hire." One of the brain's best, most powerful defense mechanisms against change is confusion. The confusion simply means, "I'm scared to see what's next." Or, "I'm scared of what I could actually do and become if I am no longer hiding behind all these fabricated 'have tos' of unpaid labor."

When this comes up, pause and breathe. Pay attention to what is happening, then lock in on the tiniest next step you can take. Maybe you need to write a clear, detailed description of what you need help with, what you will pay for that work to be done, and how often you want it done. Once you've shifted from self-sabotage to action, the noise will subside.

At this point, you'll also be tempted to sabotage your progress by telling the very people who you *know* are going to criticize your decision. This is another crafty way we hold ourselves back. No one needs to know or agree with your decision, and you certainly don't have to tell people who are going to be critical of your choices. It isn't their choice, their life, or their values.

Let's also talk about the process of individuation. Hiring help, a clear step toward financial success, is an act of individuation, the psychological process of leaving your family of origin and creating your own path through life. You don't have to leave your family physically and never see them again to become your own person. However, you do need to start making your own decisions, regardless of what you know they will say about them, especially if you know their response will be critical.

In other words, as a mentor once told me, you can love the messenger and leave the message. Keep the messages that are in alignment with your values and aspirations, and leave those that are no longer serving you.

Finally, there's a theory in law enforcement called the broken windows theory. It basically argues that in neighborhoods with broken windows, trash, and graffiti, there is more crime because people behave in ways that reflect their physical environments. I think women are hindered hugely by this same phenomenon in our homes. When there are baskets of clean clothes that aren't folded, dishes stacked from the sink all the way to the stove, when windows are dirty or bathrooms are gross, we are receiving a constant subliminal message that says, "I'm not keeping up. I'm not doing a good job. I can't even take care of my own home, so how could I ever get a promotion or do more at work?" This constant visual message is subconscious, but it is powerful, and it holds us back.

The problem isn't with us. The problem is that we have unrealistic expectations about what we can do. Having clothes piled up in baskets waiting to be washed doesn't mean you aren't capable of taking on a leadership role at work; it means you need to get some help.

3   Watch for naysayers

Naysayers are simply a reflection of our deepest fears. What is astonishing is that in this area of unpaid labor, women tend to be the *most* critical of other women who have the help they need. We senselessly attack each other with judgmental offhand comments.

As I talked to others about what kind of help they have, I had multiple women say to me with embarrassment, "Please don't tell anyone my name. I don't want everyone to know how much help I have."

Don't tell everyone that you're smart enough to have someone help you clean your house, prepare food for your family, and care for your children while you are working a big corporate job so you can be fully present with them when you get home? Don't tell anyone that someone does your laundry and puts it away so that you can have dinner with dear friends on the weekend instead of just continuing to work in a different way? Don't tell anyone that you are not going to sacrifice your own health and well-being by running yourself ragged doing two full-time jobs—one paid and one unpaid? I'm horrified that we aren't openly celebrating these choices for other women and encouraging anyone who is hesitant to hire help to do so as quickly as possible!

4   **Don't depend on husbands, wives, partners, or kids**

Another common response I hear from women about hiring help is this: "My husband would never let me do that." Or, "My partner doesn't want anyone in the house." Or, "My spouse would never spend money on that."

First, these responses beg the question: Why would a man pay someone to do work if he has someone there who will do it for free? Men typically (but not always) are better at letting other people take care of things that aren't their strengths, interests, or don't earn them money. They don't take on unpaid labor while also working full-time because they know they don't have enough time or energy, and as I said, in most cases, they don't have to because women are doing this work for them free of charge. Because of this, they may at first resist paying someone to help with household chores. Can I urge you to work through this initial resistance and not retreat to old patterns?

Ryan has not always been excited about or in favor of the help I have hired. To him, it felt frivolous and unnecessary. I've learned from our many conversations around this topic, and I have a few tips for you to help get your spouse on board.

First, sit down with your partner to talk about the idea when no one is stressed or tired. The best times for these conversations aren't when you are overflowing with resentment, exhausted from the weight of your work and all the unpaid labor you are doing, or when you are distracted with children. Schedule a dinner out, take a walk, and choose a time of the day when both of you are fresh.

Suggest a trial period of at least two or three months in length for adding help. This also serves you in hiring someone because you have an easy out if the person isn't working out as you want. I've even gone so far as to say, "Let me hire this person for a three-month trial period. Right now, let's schedule a date three months from today to assess how it's going." I have done this several times, and each time, we haven't even needed the check-in because he sees the value of having the extra help once we added it.

Next, if you have different expectations for what "clean" is in your home or for the frequency of that cleaning, do not fall for this trap. Your partner or spouse says, "I'll just start doing more. We don't need to pay money for that. I can do it." We tried this on multiple occasions, but let's be clear. My idea of clean and Ryan's couldn't be more different. I love him to pieces, but I know that when I travel for work and he is in charge, no one picks up the house or does a single dish until about three hours before I'm expected, at which time an emergency mission begins to get the house ready for me to walk through the door! While my kids love these flurries of frantic cleaning that they share with their dad every once in a while, this is not a sustainable strategy for everyday life.

Let's also address having your kids do the unpaid labor. I have a few tips here as well. If you're giving jobs to kids, tie the work to a reward that can be taken away if the work isn't done. For example, "You can play on the PS4 for one hour *after* the cleaning checklist that is hanging on the fridge is done." Or, "You can get your phone unplugged in the morning only after household jobs are done."

Confusion is one
of the most
powerful weapons
of self-sabotage.

My teenage daughter gets paid a set amount each month to do all our family laundry because I don't want her learning that unpaid labor is an expectation for girls. I deposit the money once a month (money we would probably be giving her anyhow since she is too busy with sports and extracurricular activities right now to have a job), and if the laundry isn't done, folded, and put away by Monday morning each week, I simply move a week's worth of the monthly wages out of her checking account back into mine. No fighting, no yelling, just a simple online exchange. You only get paid if you do the work! She did skip the laundry one weekend, and her incredulous, indignant response to the loss of money in her account was hilarious. I still wish I had recorded her rant about the injustice of it all! She hasn't missed a week since.

My son gets paid for every load of dishes he unloads. He keeps a tally chart on the fridge. Then I don't have to beg, and he can use this money when he wants to do something fun. Again, I'd probably be paying for those experiences anyhow, so it's awesome to at least get a household job done in exchange for that money.

You get the idea. There must be some sort of exchange if you don't want to nag and beg and yell and basically use up as much energy as if you just did it yourself. Many parents who get into this exhausting cycle tend to return to doing chores themselves because it feels so much easier than the constant battle!

5   Recognize the value of unpaid labor

If you are in a relationship where the role you have chosen is to take care of all the unpaid labor, don't you dare undervalue yourself or your contribution. If you weren't there taking care of the kids and the house, your partner could not be earning the income they bring home. Therefore, you're really earning that money too. And if you have someone in your home who is taking care of most of the unpaid labor, you better recognize their value also and be sure they feel appreciated and valued.

Conversely, if you are beating yourself up because you can't seem to figure out how to work full-time, build a thriving side business, *and* take care of all the unpaid labor in your home, *stop it!* Stop it, stop it, stop it.

There is nothing wrong with you. You simply don't have enough help.

6 Categorize this as a stewardship issue

And now, our final point to examine: categorize this as a stewardship issue. Getting help is one of the most important steps you can take to be a good steward of your unique gifts. You've got to pay people to do jobs that use their unique gifts so that you can use *your* gifts to their fullest capacity.

I was talking with my stepdad about his successful insurance business, and he said this to me: "There are very few people in this world who are producers, who can go out there and sell and create new business. There are lots of people who can be great support staff. I've known from early on that my job is to produce and to let someone else take care of the details behind the scenes."

I think so many of us *under*value the gifts we have been given. We think everyone can lead a team of people, everyone can create growth in a business, everyone can teach or train people, or everyone can coach people to life-change. I don't believe this is true. Remember how we often undervalue our areas of natural genius because they feel so easy to us?

I frequently return to the parable of the talents in the Bible. In the story, one servant was given five talents (the form of currency at the time the story was written), and he went out into the world, put his money to work, and made five more. Another servant was given three talents, and he went out and did the same, making three more. The final servant was given one talent. He dug a hole in the ground and put the master's money in it.

Even if you are familiar with the story, you might not remember why he buried his talent. He says this to his master: "I was afraid, and I went and hid your talent in the ground. See, you have what is yours."

Goodness, that gives me the chills.

I was afraid.

I was afraid of what people would think of me.

I was afraid that if I went out and really invested the talents, I might actually be great.

I was afraid I would fail if I took a risk.

I was afraid to be vulnerable and let someone help me.

I was afraid.

So I did nothing.

So many of you are beating yourselves up, saying you just don't have the time or the skills to create what you are dreaming of creating. I'm going to argue that what you're *really* afraid of is that you have five talents, and you know it. Deep down in places you don't even recognize, you know that if you stopped doing all the unpaid labor that is outside of your gifts and instead invested those talents, you might get ten talents back in return. You might even triple your investment, and that is scarier than staying in a space that you know, even if that space isn't healthy. This is about being a steward of the talents (not money, but gifts) that you have been given, your areas of natural genius.

I was at a leadership conference about ten years ago, and Pastor John Ortberg said something that went straight to the core of my being. It has become the rallying cry of my work— the summary of my life's purpose in one sentence. I will never forget where I was sitting, what I was wearing, or the shock of energy that passed through my body when he said it. He said, "If you are a woman, and God has given you the gift of leadership, then for God's sake, *lead*."

Some of you out there have been given the gift of leadership. You have been given an ambitious heart and a desire to make a difference. You aren't going to be like most people in this world. Stop burying your unique and valuable talents under dishes and laundry and all the things that allow you to avoid the work that would really change our world. Own them and step into them and let people help you do the other things so you can do the things only you can do.

CHAPTER 9 EXERCISE
UNLOAD THE UNPAID LABOR

Go back to the unpaid labor survey you took in the middle of the chapter, and choose one or two of the items on the list. You may try writing about this in your journal.

- Who can you pay to do this work for you?

- When you even consider eliminating this work from your list, what resistance comes up?

- What does that resistance have to teach you?

- Could what's being revealed actually be one of the biggest blocks to your growth and progress?

10

Surrender to Structure

I F Y O U asked my mom what I was like as a small child, she
would smile and tell you that I always embraced a higher
level of structure than most people. Even as a young girl,
I loved tracking charts, detailed processes, and clear
guidelines. I diligently used my assignment notebook in
school, had an ambitious goal poster hanging on my bedroom
wall, and I always carried around a color-coded calendar
that I used to monitor my busy schedule of family events,
practices, and games. During different seasons, I also created more targeted charts that I used to track how many
free throws I shot out in the driveway each day or how many
books I read each week. I am certain no one ever checked
out and read more books from our tiny small-town library
than I did each summer! My mom still chuckles and shakes
her head at these memories of raising a very ambitious, very
structured child!

It's obvious that embracing structure is an area of natural
genius to me, something that mostly feels easy and effortless. However, in over twenty years of leading people, I've
realized that I am *not* the norm. As a leader especially, I was

constantly baffled when people on my team didn't just follow the proven processes that had been laid out for them. I would often think to myself, "The checklist said to do this, so just *do* it. It's not that hard." Embracing structure may be my jam, but it isn't so simple for everyone!

I use the book *The Greatest Salesman in the World* by Og Mandino as an important tool with all my coaching clients. However, I was first introduced to the book *long* before I ever dreamed of becoming a business coach. I remember the day I first heard a powerful passage read aloud from the book like it was yesterday. I was sitting with my team in the front row of an annual awards ceremony wearing a sparkly black and gold floor-length formal gown. The woman on stage who had just been recognized as the top salesperson in the company for that fiscal year shared these words from the book:

I will persist until I succeed. I was not delivered unto this world in defeat, nor does failure course in my veins. I am not a sheep waiting to be prodded by my shepherd. I am a lion and I refuse to talk, to walk, to sleep with the sheep. I will hear not those who weep and complain, for their disease is contagious. Let them join the sheep. The slaughterhouse of failure is not my destiny.

I was so moved, I leaned across four people completely disregarding my big poofy gown and grabbed a pen I saw in my friend's hand. I scribbled the words "Og Mandino— Greatest Salesman" on the program I had on my lap. When I got back to my hotel room that night, I ordered the book. *The Greatest Salesman in the World* was at my house when I got home from the event, and I started reading it immediately. About fifty pages in, there are ten scrolls. These are two-to-three-page writings containing core principles that are designed to change your habits of thinking, which lead to changes in your behavior, and eventually, the words in these scrolls are designed to change your entire life. They certainly have changed mine.

Scroll #1 contains the powerful instructions to read each scroll for thirty days in a prescribed manner before proceeding to the next: first, read the scroll in silence after waking in the morning; then again in silence after lunch; and finally, read the words again at day's end, just before going to sleep, but this time I was to read the words aloud. As someone with an unusual proclivity for embracing structure, I never even considered another option. My plan would be to do as Mandino recommended for each of the ten scrolls.

So, for the next thirty days, I read Scroll #1 in the morning, after lunch, and out loud to myself before I went to bed. Then I proceeded to Scroll #2. Next, I dug into Scroll #3, and I worked through all ten scrolls over the next ten months. The first time it occurred to me that most people do *not* buy books like *The Greatest Salesman in the World* and do *exactly* as they instruct was when I stayed in a hotel room with my mom and our friend Celine about four months into this new daily discipline. When it was time to get ready for bed, I pulled out my book and they giggled as I read my scroll to them like it was a bedtime story. In the end, they didn't mind too much, and we still chuckle together, remembering them tucked into their beds like little girls as I read to them aloud each night.

That year, as I continued to read my scrolls three times a day, my team and I had our best year in sales *by far*. I earned my first incentive trip to Germany, and I almost doubled the size of my organization. This simple daily interaction with Og Mandino's scrolls incrementally changed my habits of thinking, which changed my behaviors and the results showed.

The words have continued to change the trajectory of my life, and they are still a part of my daily routine, though now I only read one in the morning to start my day.

Almost ten years later, when I decided to work with my first coach, he mailed me all of the materials we would be using in our work together, including a fresh copy of *The Greatest Salesman in the World.* I was thrilled. During our first session, he asked me to interact with one of the scrolls three times a day. I enthusiastically said, "I know those scrolls well—I've done them before. They completely transformed my business!"

He offhandedly said, "Oh, yes, you've read them? It is a really famous book."

I quickly corrected him. "No, I *really* worked through them ... like it says in the book to do ... each scroll for thirty days, three times a day." It took me a *long* time to convince him that I really had done the scrolls exactly as instructed in the book for ten months! He assures me that to this day, even having worked with thousands of clients using the scrolls, I am the only one he has ever met who has done this on her own. Like I said, my proclivity for embracing structure certainly *isn't* the norm!

I want to emphasize that if you are someone more like me, a person who loves structure, you're going to lead and work with a ton of people who don't. Most people do not naturally think or act like you. Structure is not their superpower, and it never will be. Your goal is to learn to help teach them to find small, simple structures they can implement, not to expect them to operate like you do. It took me a long season of constant disappointment and frustration before I realized that my expectations for the people I led weren't realistic. As I frequently remind my clients about their areas of natural genius, "You are not normal. You are amazing, and beyond exceptional in your performance in your areas of genius, but you are not the norm. The people you lead won't think like you."

Conversely, if you are a person for whom structure does *not* come easily, I want to assure you that my goal is not to make you like me. I will challenge some of the mindsets you have around structure, and I will dig into why you resist structure so vehemently. I may even warm you up to the idea of structure a bit, but my main goal is to help you discover the structures that will support your natural strengths.

Structure Gets a Bad Rap

Let's start with the overarching idea of structure. Without thinking about it too much, I want you to write in the margins of this book, in your journal, or maybe in a note on your phone the first word that comes to mind when you hear the word *structure*.

When I ask most people, especially entrepreneurs, what they think of structure, they will almost immediately say words like *rigid, restricting, boring, frustrating*, or *confining*. Some will even physically react in a posture of defense, sort of hunching their shoulders and wincing, as if to say, "I *know* I should like it or embrace it, but *yuck*!"

Many also have a lot of guilt or shame attached to the idea of structure. They think they *should* be embracing structure more than they do, but they just can't seem to sustain long periods of what feels like unenjoyable rigidity. They'll try to stick to a new system or habit for a stretch, maybe embracing a budget or adhering to some sort of time management tool, but eventually, exhausted from the constant internal fight with themselves, they give up and retreat. After a while, it starts to feel like embracing any kind of structure leads to almost certain failure, so they don't even bother trying.

If this feeling of constant shame or hopelessness around structure resonates with you, or if your entire being recoils at even the thought of implementing a new structure because you know you won't stick with it, I'm here to help. However, before we start to work on shifting your mindset about the concept as a whole, let's start by identifying the spaces in which you are most resistant to it.

Structure Self-Evaluation

Let's look at the five areas of our lives where structure or a lack of it causes the most frustration and pain:

- health
- money
- time
- business or work
- relationships

I want you to take a second right now and rank yourself in each of these areas on a scale of one to ten. This number doesn't have to do with structure specifically; I just want you to evaluate how you are doing in each of these areas. Are you thriving (ten)? Struggling (one)?

For example, let's look at health. Are you eating food that fuels your body intentionally and consistently throughout the day? Are you in a regular routine of physical activity that supports your immune system and your heart and lungs? A ranking of one in this area would mean that if you continue down the path you are on, there are going to be serious health consequences, maybe even in the immediate future. A ten

Structure has firm boundaries, but living with structure does not have to be restrictive.

would mean that you are nailing it. While maybe you're not perfect, you regularly exercise, your food choices are fueling your body and providing great energy, and you just went to the doctor and got a clean bill of health. This area of life is humming along like a well-oiled machine. Take a moment to rank all five areas before moving on.

Now, let's look at the areas with a score above six. What structures are in place that support this area? If you are looking at health, for example, do you have healthy, consistent habits of grocery shopping and meal planning and prepping each week? Do you have a regular workout schedule that you follow at home or at a gym or a group of friends with whom you exercise regularly?

Even relationships, which you wouldn't first think depend on structure, thrive within it. Marriages and committed life partnerships flourish in the structure of regular date nights, celebrations of anniversaries, and scheduled time together to connect and talk. When these structures aren't in place, relationships tend to grow distant, and the people within them lose their connection.

Now, I want you to look at the areas where you ranked yourself less than five. Are there structures in place to support them? These tend to be the areas where we make commitments to structure, keep them for a short time, and then drift back to old habits—often without even noticing or consciously thinking about it, or as soon as we experience a disruption in our routine like a vacation or sick day.

Don't worry. Remember, I'm not here to force you into rigid rules or systems you have to follow so that you can improve your rankings. Rather, I'm going to educate you about the mindsets that allow us to embrace structure so that you can release the resistance, observe yourself in moments of decision, and, hopefully, begin to surrender to structure.

Seven Beliefs about Structure

I've identified seven beliefs I have about structure that allow me to wholeheartedly embrace it. If you just try to change your behaviors without addressing these deeper mindsets, the changes you make in any area will continue to be fleeting.

1   Structure is not a restrictive cage; it is the path to freedom.

2   Structure protects us from the inefficiency of multitasking.

3   The most powerful enemy of structure is the expectation of perfection.

4   Embracing structure *requires* rest from it.

5   At one edge of structure is mastery; at the other is loss of freedom.

6   Surrendering to structure feels awkward and uncomfortable.

7   You will never fully embrace structure until you recognize that your value is separate from your performance.

Let's unpack these ideas a little and explore how to apply them.

1   **Structure is not a restrictive cage;
    it is the path to freedom**
Structure has boundaries that are firm, but the experience of living within it does not have to be restrictive. Structure actually creates a safe haven for productive action and progress. Resisting structure can be thought of like two foes squaring off in a boxing ring. On one side of the ring, you have structure, and on the opposite side, diametrically opposed, there is freedom. Your thought habits often want to pit these two

against one another, and this leads you to believe you can only have one or the other. You can have structure *or* you can have freedom. There must be a winner in the battle.

In contrast, people like me who embrace structure tend to think of structure as being like gravity, which keeps us safe and grounded on Earth and allows us to move, create, grow, and change. Gravity keeps us safe while we are in action, living our lives. We don't walk around saying, "I wish I didn't have this stupid gravity pressing on me all the time. It's so restricting and keeps me tied down to the ground." Without it, we would all float off into space, disconnected and in constant danger.

Structure doesn't limit our creativity; it gives us the freedom to create. Historically, some of the world's greatest artists embraced some sort of structure within which they expressed their artistic genius. Professional writers typically block out time each day to write, or they write a certain number of words or pages each day. In his memoir titled *On Writing*, author Stephen King describes his creative system: "If I don't write every day, the characters begin to stale off in my mind... I begin to lose my hold on the story's plot and pace." King likes to write ten pages a day. Over a three-month span, that amounts to around 180,000 words. "The first draft of a book—even a long one—should take no more than three months, the length of a season," he notes. If you spend too long on your piece, King believes the story begins to take on an odd, unfamiliar feel, which becomes detrimental to the plot.

Michelangelo, one of the great Renaissance artists, most famous for his painting on the ceiling of the Sistine Chapel and his statue of David in Florence, also created his art within structure. He had deadlines, he had a budget, and he had tools to keep organized. When sculpting David, he first created a wax model of his design and submerged it in water. As he worked, he would lower the water level and sculpt what he could see emerging in the model. This structure guided each step of his creative process. He also didn't just work when the creative spirits moved him. He worked consistently each day for a certain number of hours in order to meet the deadline for the commissioned piece. It took him three years working in this way to finish the marble masterpiece. Indeed, even one of our world's most celebrated artists embraced a high level of structure.

2 **Structure protects us from the inefficiency of multitasking**

A study done at the University of California, Irvine found that every time you shift the focus of your brain from a project to an email or a text or some other notification, it takes twenty-three minutes and fifteen seconds to get back to your original level of focus. That's right—more than twenty-three minutes! Can you believe it? So, if I'm typing this chapter and I get a text, stop to read and respond, and then come back to my writing, it takes me *twenty-three minutes* to get back to where I was before. That is a staggering realization.

Next, an important scientific fact: our brains *cannot* multitask. We often joke or brag that we are the best at multitasking, but this is just not true. Every scientific study ever done about the human brain agrees that our brains are incapable of thinking about more than one thing at a time. When we *think* we are multitasking, we are actually quickly shifting our focus from one task to another, which makes us *less* effective at both things! It also creates anxiety to constantly switch our attention back and forth. There are most likely a multitude of causes for rising anxiety rates in our world, but I believe our constant "multitasking" is a significant contributor.

Also, when you're shifting your attention back and forth between different tasks, what happens to your heart rate? Does it race like mine? Do you sometimes get a headache? Do you feel foggy or like your brain is swirling? Do you ever feel like you're more tired than you should be at certain points in the day? That's because your brain is in overdrive, switching points of focus repeatedly over a stretch of time. Locking your brain into one task will allow you to get more done in less time with significantly less energy.

3 The most powerful enemy of structure is the expectation of perfection

Every January 1, most people take a deep breath and evaluate their lives. It's the beginning of the new year. Now is the time to make changes and to embrace structure in the areas of life that have plagued us for so long. It is time to commit to structure.

Almost immediately after making this new commitment, we begin to follow a habit of thinking about structure that is completely unrealistic and rooted in fantasy. We say things like, "Starting today, I am going to go to the gym five days a week." Or we might announce, "I am going to start every single day with an hour of quiet, reading, and reflection." And of course, we are all familiar with the two most popular commitments of changing our eating habits drastically and following a budget to a penny. The unrealistic expectation behind each of these? Perfection.

Remember my client Tina, who does really well in her life and work when she uses a Six Most Important Things List each day? She logically knows that this simple tool is beneficial. She has seen its effects first hand. However, even Tina, during a busy stretch of parenting and running a growing business, will periodically stop embracing this structure. She will commit to writing out her list each day at the start of a week or month. Then, a few days later, she will inevitably miss a day. Life gets in the way. Employee situations arise. She forgets her notebook at home. She has a sick child home from school. The reasons don't even really matter. Here's what does matter. Her brain immediately starts saying to her, "This isn't working. You are failing. You can't even stick with this simple process for a week. You might as well give up on these daily lists and just wing it again." Her thought habits frame her efforts as a *failure*. And what does she do when confronted with this imminent and continuous prospect of what her subconscious mind defines as failure? She chucks the list for the rest of the week.

I'd like to shine a spotlight on these tiny, often unnoticed but critical moments of choice. Do I frame this lack of structure on one day as *failure*, beat myself up about it, tell myself all the reasons I'm never going to be able to succeed, feel guilty, then have to recover from all the self-flagellation, and, finally, surrender and recommit? Or do I not give it a second thought and say to myself, "Dang—I didn't get to my list today, but there is no need for perfection; time to make my list for tomorrow"?

If the expectation is perfection, you will most likely quit altogether. If the expectation is imperfect progress, you won't think twice about a missed day or two. You'll just pick up where you left off, and you will save all the emotional energy it takes to recover from your own unmet expectations. Imagine how much of this saved energy you could devote to the efforts of creation if you weren't constantly battling an unrealistic expectation of perfection.

Structure does not require perfection, no matter what our demanding thought habits tell us. I can't tell you how many people sigh deeply with relief when they find out that

If you dig deeply
in the areas where
you are resisting
structure, you will
find unhealed pain.

even those people most committed to structure do it very imperfectly. Perfect is an unattainable standard. There is no success or failure in embracing structure. There are only daily choices.

4   **Embracing structure *requires* rest from it**
Expecting that every element of every day of your life will be structured is unrealistic and unhealthy and ignores our need for rhythms. We need structure, and then we need rest. Simply put, there is no way to sustain structure over the long haul if you do not have a break from it.

If you ask people who stick to a budget successfully, most have built in "fun money" with which they can do whatever they want. If you ask people who work out consistently, most find a number of workouts a week that feels like it fits for their life, and they do that, but they typically don't work out every single day at the exact same time. They also rest. Sustainable structure happens in a rhythm.

Let's look again at an area of life where you want or need to embrace a higher level of structure: health, money, time, business/work, or relationships. Look at your goals in that area. Are they realistic? Do they take into account rhythms and rest? If not, you probably won't be able to sustain the behavior change for longer than a few weeks or months. Surrendering to structure is quite the opposite of forcing yourself to submit to rigid rules and guidelines. It is not controlling or fighting oneself. Embracing structure is one of the greatest outward acts of self-love.

This is especially important when taking care of our bodies, and it is exactly why the structure of dieting does not work for a lifetime. When you deny yourself, fight your body's natural need to survive, and put an exorbitant amount of energy into keeping yourself under control, you are basically living in a constant state of battle. Eventually, you get tired, and you lose, returning to old habits that no longer serve you.

Eating psychology coach Emily LaVoie describes this pattern like a pendulum. When you pull yourself so far to one side of restriction with food, at some point, you grow weary and let go. Then you usually swing all the way to the other side and overindulge. The swing can happen each day or over weeks or months, but each time you swing, you then have to recover from the feeling of failure before recommitting. This is exhausting and damaging to our self-esteem. Also, at the root of this approach is fear, or lack of trust in oneself.

Again, the surrender to structure flows from a space of love. I love myself; therefore, I choose to live in a way that cherishes my one and only body. When I don't make choices that honor my body, I don't feel very good. I then choose to return to the space of caring for myself because I recognize my own value and love myself enough to do so. When I choose to indulge, I enjoy the meal thoroughly and those with whom I am eating. Then I simply choose to return to structure the next day. This has nothing to do with shame or guilt. This is not you versus you. This is about you *loving* you, so you choose to surrender to structure. Sustainable structure requires rest from it.

5   At one edge of structure is mastery; at the other is loss of freedom

When I think of a person's willingness to embrace structure, I imagine a line of continuum on which the highest levels of focused structure are on one side. Focused structure at the highest levels creates mastery. Think about the focused structure by which an Olympic athlete lives as an example. Every morsel of food they eat, every minute they sleep, every hour of practice—all is orchestrated and controlled to ensure the best result. Or think of NBA players like LeBron James and Steph Curry, who live and operate in a highly structured environment, controlling every single element of their lives from the weights they lift to the food they eat to how they warm up before games so that they can perform at such a high level.

Or what about someone like a CEO of a major corporation or even the president of the United States? Their time is structured and controlled down to the minute, usually by someone else whose sole purpose is to fight to keep only the most important issues in front of that leader. These leaders have people preparing their food, buying gifts for their loved ones, spending millions of dollars to ensure their safety, and basically taking care of all their daily needs so that they can focus on the important work of leadership. In other words, they surrender to structure instead of doing hours of unpaid labor. Their lives are *very* structured because they hold the most powerful level of influence in a company, a country, or even in the world. Those who are masters at anything must embrace the most rigorous levels of structure.

MASTERY   **LOSS OF FREEDOM**

The Highest Levels of   Complete Disregard
Focused Structure   for Structure

At the opposite end of the continuum is where you'll find a complete disregard for structure. This always leads to the thing people who resist structure fear most—loss of freedom. If a person refuses to embrace structure in any area of life for long enough, structure will eventually impose itself on them.

For example, if you ignore structure in your finances completely and don't track your spending or saving or what you are earning, you could go bankrupt, end up on welfare, and then the government will take control over how much money you earn. It is a structure imposed on you by someone else. If you don't sleep adequately for a long time, and you ignore the structure of a reasonable bedtime, your body will eventually get sick, essentially forcing you into the structure you have been avoiding. Then you *must* rest. Structure is imposing itself on you, and you have lost your freedom.

Obviously, in each of these examples, there are instances in which the circumstances that lead us to needing assistance are out of our control. There are reasons someone ends up in a hospital that aren't connected to how well they have taken care of themselves. There are also reasons a person might end up on welfare that don't have anything to do with their inability to embrace structure. However, in so many instances, our resistance to structure does result in structure being imposed on us. It is a myth that the opposite of freedom is structure. The more we resist structure because we feel like it is infringing on our freedom, the closer we get to the most extreme loss of freedom.

6 **Surrendering to structure
feels awkward and uncomfortable**

A few years ago, my business coach Pamela Slim recommended I read a book by Mike Michalowicz called *Profit First*. She challenged me to not just read the book but to really follow the "profit first" method of running the finances of my businesses. I'm always up for a challenge, and I love the idea of more profit from any business I own, so I ordered the book and dug in. The first few chapters were *awesome*. I totally loved the premise of the structure Michalowicz was encouraging entrepreneurs to use, and while I have cleaned up many of my unhealthy financial habits over twenty years of building a business, I knew I could do better. I was all in. Correction—I was all in *until* the chapter on checking accounts, when I really had to start to act. Michalowicz even says at this point in the book, "What you are about to do is the foundation of *Profit First*. This is the structure your profits will be built on. All the muscle in the world is useless if it isn't connected to a strong skeletal structure. These accounts are the bones."

The first step is simply to open five checking accounts for your business and to name them Income, Profit, Owner's Compensation, Tax, and OPEX (operating expenses). That's it. I had opened checking accounts before, and it wasn't particularly difficult to do, but my response to this simple instruction was *fierce*.

Together, Ryan and I own three businesses... so, I need fifteen checking accounts? *Fifteen* checking accounts? That's a little crazy. What bank would I go to where I'm going to ask to open that many accounts? Will they all have to be business checking accounts with all the fees? How will I track all of this in QuickBooks? I don't even know how to add a new account to QuickBooks. My bookkeeper and my accountant are going to freak out. We already have too many checking accounts between all the businesses and our personal accounts and rentals. Is the bank even open today? I'm going to be out of town for the next four days. And *really*? For *each* business I need *five*? Come on.

This is just a *taste* of what resistance to structure can sound like. My head was literally spinning. And remember, this is from a person who loves structure! So, guess what I did? I emailed the author directly. I seriously did. I was going to show him, creator of a proven system and author of the bestselling book, that I knew better. Surely, I didn't need fifteen accounts. Surely, I could do it my own way and get a similar result. When we first talked about the book, my coach said she knew Mike, so I included her name in the email that read:

> Hey Mike!
>
> Pam Slim recommended your book and I'm LOVING it!
> Quick question—I own three businesses.
> Do I really need fifteen checking accounts?
> Sort of makes my head spin . . . not gonna lie. LOL. ☺
>
> Amy

To my surprise, even though it was four o'clock on a Friday afternoon, I got an email response right back with a video of Mike Michalowicz talking *just* to me. This is what he said:

> Amy Kemp! It's head spin time! Regarding three businesses, yes, five accounts per business. Don't let your head spin. If we meld the businesses together, meaning if you share accounts for the businesses, it gets really confusing, and you don't know which one is a profit center and which one may not be . . . I know the idea makes your head spin. Trust the process. I swear to you it will work. Follow the system, and you're going to get very clear on what business is doing well. Maybe all three of them are, but then you'll see to what degree each one is.
>
> Hope that helps! Have a great weekend!

Well *crap*. He wasn't going to let me off the hook, and he was even nice about it! There was no way to avoid embracing this structure. But did I open the checking accounts? Nope. Enter the next level of resistance in my brain. Here's what it sounded like in round two!

What if I go to all this trouble and it doesn't work? What if I open all these accounts and I don't stick with the system? I haven't even read the whole book. Maybe I should do that before I really act on anything? Maybe I need to talk to my accountant first? Or my husband? Yes, I should definitely ask a few people to affirm this decision before I really jump in. There are so many existing structures in place that are going to have to get torn down before I build this new structure, and that is going to be a mess. There are other accounts already—I'll have to rename them and move the money in them. This is going to be a *huge* undertaking...

Stay tuned for the conclusion of the story! But first, I must pause to point out a few important observations. The process of embracing any kind of new structure in your life feels overwhelming at first. There are *tons* of tiny steps. Not everyone will understand why you're doing it. It will take more time and money than you think it will. New structure feels awkward, inconvenient, and uncomfortable. It *is* a mess. But it's very likely that what you are doing now is, too, and on the other side of the new structure you are implementing is what you're really looking for: freedom, joy, and contentment.

Also, I don't think we always take the emotional experience of embracing a new structure into account when we decide to step into change, which makes it way worse when the inevitable mess of transition arrives. The process of creating a new structure is slow. It's awkward. *But*... once it's in place and running, man is it worth it.

7 **You will never fully embrace structure until you recognize that your value is separate from your performance**
Here's how the minds of most people operate: "If I follow this often newly instituted structure perfectly, I am a *success*. If I don't, I am a *failure*." Performance—followed by an

evaluation of the performance—leads to a conclusion that is deeply connected to your value as a person. Mix a smidge of perfectionism into the experience, and you've delivered a nice sucker punch to your self-esteem.

For some reason, we don't say to ourselves, "I succeeded at implementing this new structure." Or "I failed at implementing this new structure." We say, "I am a success." Or "I am a failure." And when we connect the very essence of our value to our performance in any way, we are in dangerous territory.

I want you to imagine you have the words *value* and *performance* written on the palms of your hands.

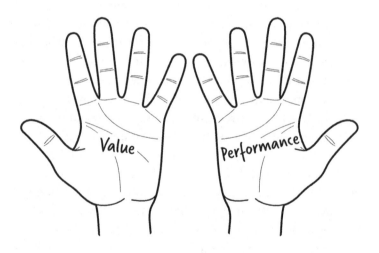

When value and performance are linked, it's as if our hands are clasped together tightly and are inseparable. We cannot create anything with our hands locked together in a vise grip. We become paralyzed by the connection of these two things.

This linking of value and performance suggests to us such nonsensical thinking as "If I fail at something, I am intrinsically a failure." If this is true, I won't take chances. I won't try new things. I won't play around with possible variations of a plan. I won't put myself in the space of rejection. At the root of this kind of thinking is this belief: *if I perform* perfectly, *I am valuable.* What an unrealistic expectation for yourself! You don't stand a chance against that thought habit.

I'd like to share an exercise that I use with clients that smashes this unhealthy connection between performance and value to smithereens. Start your day holding your hands tightly clasped in a prayer posture, as if your value and performance are connected. As you read the statements below, slowly and intentionally separate your two hands, reminding yourself that you are free to succeed and free to fail because your performance is not tied to your value. They are two very separate entities. You are valuable no matter what happens in the day ahead. Recognize that your hands, now separate, are in a posture of surrender, and they are able to receive and to create.

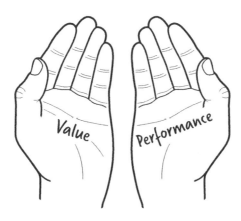

Here are the words to read as you unclasp your hands and open them to receive and create:

My value is unconditional. Nothing I do or don't do can subtract from my intrinsic value as a person. There are no conditions placed on my value. The truth is very simple. I am; therefore, I am of value.

My performance does not affect my value. My performance in any area of my life does not increase or decrease my intrinsic value. I am not what I do or how well I perform. I simply am, and that is enough. When I make this distinction and keep my performance separate from my value, I am free to create and work without pressure or fear.

I am unique. No one else in the world can create what I am supposed to create. I have a blend of talents and gifts that are mine and mine alone. The more I celebrate and use them, the more the world benefits. I have everything I need to fulfill my unique calling in life.

Beneath Resistance to Structure, You Will Find Unhealed Pain

This final thought about structure is deep and so vital. I stumbled upon it quite accidentally as I continued to work through *Profit First*. In the book, Michalowicz explains that most entrepreneurs become slaves to their businesses, which become, as he calls them, "giant, scary, soul-sucking, cash-eating monsters." The system he created shifts from the normal business accounting formula of "Sales – Expenses = Profit" to a restructured flow of money through the business where you set aside profit for yourself *first*, then pay expenses and remove the temptation of overspending.

The process logically made all the sense in the world to me. As my businesses continue to grow, I want to be a good steward of the incoming financial resources. In addition, as I mentioned earlier, my trusted coach had high praise for the system and had many clients happily and successfully using it. Bottom line—I *knew*, in my conscious brain, that the system worked. I mean, what business owner doesn't want to earn more from a business? But for some reason, I could not move forward with it.

One week passed. I didn't do anything.

And another week passed. I didn't take action.

Third week? Still nothing.

Then, in the fourth week, I had a call with my coach that unearthed some things that still feel vulnerable and raw. Together, we discovered the source of my resistance.

About ten years ago, I went through a season of being a leader and business owner that was deeply challenging financially and emotionally. In rank and recognition, my business appeared to be thriving—there was growth, I was moving up the career path in title—but for a myriad of reasons outside of my control, my income dropped suddenly and significantly.

I can remember coming home from an event late one night wearing a new suit jacket that signified my new prestigious rank. Hundreds of people from my organization attended, and it was, by all external accounts, an amazing event full of positive energy. In contrast, I was emotionally and physically drained from the stresses of having everything look great while simultaneously feeling crushed by the weight of the financial burden of providing enough income for our family. I sat down on the floor of my office that night and started hot gluing googly eyes to tubes of hand creams to make them look like little snowmen. I desperately needed the cash I would earn from selling these fifteen-dollar holiday gifts, or I wasn't sure how I would pay our mortgage that month. Frustrated and deeply ashamed, tears rolled down my face as I thought, "What am I doing wrong? I just led a meeting filled with hundreds of people who I've taught how to sell these products. I thought by now I wouldn't have to do this kind of work anymore. But here I am, working so hard, and it's still not enough."

What made it especially painful is that during that season no one knew publicly what I was experiencing privately. I had a "perfect" façade that everyone saw, but behind the scenes, I was terrified every day. While the realities of fighting for financial survival have passed, the aftereffects of that difficult season have been long-lasting.

As I described that memory and several others like it to my coach, she used the word *traumatic* to describe some of the experiences I had. Traumatic? That seemed a little extreme. Maybe things had been difficult, but I brushed aside the idea of trauma quickly, thinking about how many blessings I had in my life and about how so many people experience trauma that is so much more painful and life-altering than this one season of financial strain. But Pam persisted during our conversation, and as I described how I was resisting taking action on these simple *Profit First* steps, I realized she was probably right. Again, even though the thought of implementing changes to our financial systems was triggering me, even though logically there was no risk at all, I could *physically* feel the fear pressing on my chest and making my heart race. I never wanted to be that financially vulnerable again.

Still today, I can easily respond to financial pressures and decisions using survival-inspired actions that I learned during this struggle. For example, I recently made a silly error transferring money from the wrong account in my online banking, and one of my accounts was overdrawn. I had *plenty* of money in all accounts. It was an innocent

My performance
in any area of my
life does not increase
or decrease
my intrinsic value.

mistake, but my response was much stronger than the situation warranted. I opened my online banking, saw a number in red on the screen, and instantly my body went crazy. My heart started racing, I broke out in a sweat, and there was this deep pressure on my chest, like something was pushing on my heart. I found myself barely able to breathe.

Without even time to think, my body returned to that season of my life when I was so scared every day to open the online banking because I wasn't sure if I had enough to make it through the week or even the day. It returned me to how I felt on that floor hot gluing googly eyes onto hand creams. Even though our financial situation is completely different now and I had nothing to fear, and the transfer was a simple fixable mistake, physically and emotionally, I *felt* the same fear, the same panic, all the things I experienced ten years ago.

Pam challenged me to explore my stress responses when facing anything that brings up that feeling of fear and panic. What do I do when I start to feel that way? What is my default coping mechanism? Usually, I put my head down and get crazy busy doing work that doesn't pay me what I am worth and that isn't at all my calling in life. Again, cue gluing googly eyes onto hand creams. I also tend to blame myself for the lack of income, thinking that I didn't follow the budget closely enough, or, even worse, I feel like there is something wrong with me that I cannot create the money we need. These thoughts are like a battering ram to my self-esteem.

This book, this structure of *Profit First* being right in my face, was revealing what still needed healing inside of me. The thought of implementing this new structure was bringing forward something I had shoved down so deep I didn't even consciously know it was there. It also brought to the surface the embarrassment and shame of that time in my life. The fear of *survival*. The feeling of being inauthentic and faking it publicly and having to put on a good front, when behind the scenes I felt like I was drowning. That's when it dawned on me. I wasn't resisting the structure because I am resistant to structure or couldn't follow the simple system. I was resisting the structure because being in that financial space made me feel exposed and vulnerable. There was unhealed pain and loads of unprocessed emotions. I could force myself into submission in this area because I do have a tremendous amount of willpower and self-discipline. I could do it for a while, maybe even years, but eventually, to embrace and surrender to this structure, I was going to have to deal with the deep-down pain. No short cuts, no magic wands, no quick fixes. I had to heal.

After my initial conversation with Pam where my unhealed pain was acknowledged in a safe space for the first time, I walked into my office. With *zero* internal resistance, with absolutely no doubt or excuses, I simply called the bank. Within an hour, I had all the new checking accounts set up, and we were on our way to running my business finances in a new way. I didn't force myself. I was no longer scared or confused. I didn't feel an ounce of resistance.

As new things trigger anxious feelings about money, I continue to journal and talk about them in a safe space. I don't need anyone to fix anything. I just need a neutral ear to listen, so I can process the pain of those experiences. I still sometimes feel angry, frustrated, sad, or ashamed. If I acknowledge these emotions and allow them to pass through me freely, I can then move forward again without resistance.

I've also learned to talk directly to the Amy with the hot glue gun and googly eyes in her hands on that office floor. When she gets scared, I often remind her, "You are safe. I won't ever put you in a situation like that again. The lessons you have learned are powerful and lasting. You are worthy.

You did nothing wrong. You deserve to receive what you are currently receiving. There is no need for fear."

In summary, I surrendered to structure. I surrendered to the pain of the past, acknowledged it, felt it, and held it. Then I let it go, palms wide open with value and performance nowhere near each other. That allowed me to embrace the structure that will take my life and business to a new level of success. It's time to stop fighting yourself or trying to get yourself to embrace structure. It's time to stop giving your past story power over your present. Find the deepest root of the resistance. Pull it out, look at it, touch it, feel it, and then let it go.

It's time to *fully surrender* to structure.

Now, I want to gently invite you to take a fresh look at the areas of your life where you resist structure the most. Is it simply because you are rebellious or lack discipline, or is there more to it? I think of this kind of internal exploration, like a person walking on the beach with a metal detector. When the wand finds something metal beneath the surface, it beeps and then the person holding it stops and digs down right in that spot to find what is causing the beeping. Usually what they discover is not as valuable a find as the loud beeping would suggest! It can often be dug up, inspected, and thrown away.

Nonetheless, this excavation process is very important when it comes to understanding why you are resisting any kind of structure. Instead of fighting yourself, pushing through, or trying to find a more creative way to get yourself to embrace the structure you are resisting, stop. Dig deep right there and see what you find. I bet that when you dig deeply in the areas where you are resisting structure, you will find unhealed pain. And then your healing work can begin.

CHAPTER 10 EXERCISE
DISCOVERY QUESTIONS

Review the scores you gave yourself in each of the areas of health, money, time, business, and relationships at the start of this chapter, and answer the following questions in your journal:

- If you could only make changes in one of the five areas where your resistance to structure shows up most, which would make the greatest impact on your life? What is the smallest step of progress you could take in this area to get started?

- If you continue in your current patterns of behavior in the area in which you gave yourself the lowest score, what are some potential negative consequences in the next year? How about in the next five years? How about ten or even twenty years? Will the consequences of your behavior potentially result in a loss of freedom that is more dramatic than what you will experience by embracing structure in that area now?

- What is the smallest form of structure you could implement in this area to start to make changes?

- In the area where you struggle to embrace structure the most, can you backtrack to any experiences where you may still have unhealed pain? Instead of fighting through your resistance, can you surrender to some deeper healing work in this area?

I'd also encourage you to spend some time journaling your answers or about your own experiences in the one area where you gave yourself the lowest score.

Conclusion

RESPECT THE MILE

M Y PLAN was never to run my first marathon in my forties, but sometimes things don't work out like we plan. Life holds many surprises.

In the spring of 2018, Steve Spear, who works for World Vision, a well-known nonprofit organization, came and spoke at our church. First, he told his own inspiring story about his transformation from someone who hadn't ever even run a 5K to someone who ran from coast to coast across the entire United States. His journey was the equivalent of running a marathon per day for weeks and weeks on end. After sharing his personal story, he issued a bold invitation to everyone in our congregation. He challenged us to join the church's World Vision team and to run the Chicago Marathon to raise money that would provide clean drinking water for underprivileged children around the world.

Now, I love a challenge, particularly one with a meaningful purpose. I loved Steve's story, and I wanted to support the cause of World Vision. But throughout my athletic career— even as a collegiate basketball player—long-distance running had not agreed with my legs and feet. I had lots of issues with shin splints and tendonitis, and while I'm healthy and strong,

I don't have the lean, lithe body structure of most people I know who run. I certainly have not ever described or thought of myself as a runner. The longest I had ever run in my life was an eight-mile race, one time, many years before.

As Steve talked that morning at church, I didn't visualize myself crossing the finish line with my hands held up in victory. I didn't feel a pull in my spirit that I often do when presented with a compelling challenge. Nothing in me that morning said, "You should run the marathon." Nothing. In fact, I didn't even go to the meeting after the service ended where he explained the running plan and asked people to officially sign up for the team. I was *not* interested in running a marathon.

What I *did* do, however, was reach out to a couple of friends who *had* decided to run with World Vision. I asked them to email me the training plan they'd gotten at the meeting. I was bored with my workouts, and the spring weather was finally getting warmer. I thought I would shake it up a bit and see if I could follow the first few weeks of the training plan. I *truly* never even planned to make it through half of the scheduled runs. I got a copy of the plan from my friend, and I invited my neighbor to join me in following it for a few weeks.

My invitation text to my neighbor read, "Before you say no outright to my invitation, be clear that we are NOT running a marathon. I don't even want to run a marathon. I just thought we could follow the running schedule and it would challenge us a bit! I'm bored with my workouts." We said some variation of these words probably a hundred times over the next six months, "We do *not* have to run a marathon. We aren't even planning to run a marathon. We are simply running the distance that is on the schedule for today!"

On the first Monday of the training, we did what was on the plan and alternated running and walking for a specified length of time. The next day, we did what was on the plan for that day. Not once did we do more than what was on the sheet, even if that day's assignment felt really easy. We just stuck to the plan, doing what it said each day.

Pretty soon, we were several months into the training plan, and we started to ask each other curious questions during our runs: "What if we really ran the marathon? Is it too late to register? Are we even free that weekend? Do you think we could really do it? Would our bodies hold up? Would we have time to fundraise?" But even as we tossed around the idea of actually running the race, when it came time to hit the streets, we would again matter-of-factly remind each other, "We do *not* have to run a marathon; we will simply run the distance that is on the schedule for today!"

At some point in June, we made some phone calls to World Vision to see if running the marathon was even a possibility since we had missed the official deadline in the spring. It turned out that we were able to claim the registrations of a couple of people who had gotten injured and weren't going to be able to run after all. By midsummer, about halfway through the training plan, we were fully committed. We were going to run in the Chicago Marathon in October.

It wasn't all smooth sailing as we took the next step and the next. There were plenty of obstacles. In July, I got salmonella, and I was so dehydrated and had such a high fever that I was hospitalized twice. I couldn't work or even get off the couch for almost two full weeks. When I finally recovered, guess what I did? I went back to the plan. Those first runs after being sick were difficult and slower than our usual pace, but not impossible. Even through that comeback, I just kept focusing on each individual day of the training plan.

Over the six months of training, I had to wake up earlier than I ever have in my life to fit runs in around kids' games, school schedules, and family commitments because to do some of the longer runs at the pace we were running takes a *long time*. Often, my neighbor and I were meeting to start our runs at four thirty in the morning so we could get home, shower, and hustle to an out-of-town baseball tournament or basketball game.

At the risk of oversharing, I have to give you a few "behind the curtain" peeks at the marathon training experience. Most horrifying is that I pooped in places one would never dream of pooping during our many runs because for whatever reason, when I run long distances, my digestive system consistently does a complete and total cleanse! It was gross, but thankfully, most of our longer runs were on a trail at a nearby state park, so when nature called, I was able to find some privacy right there in nature!

I also felt *real* fear as the runs got longer. I just wasn't sure my legs could go that far without serious injury or debilitating pain. Was this even possible for my forty-two-year-old body? Would some stress-induced injury emerge as a result of the constant pounding on my legs? Then, one day, I almost stepped on a snake on the trail. For real. A snake. Now, it was only about six inches long, but it was a snake, and I am *not* a fan of snakes. If you live in the Chicagoland area and heard a scream around eight in the morning on a Thursday in mid-September of 2018, that was me, encountering an unwelcome slithering surprise!

I had also booked a week-long coaching experience with a group of clients in Italy for September because, if you remember, I was *not* planning to run a marathon. The international work trip just happened to fall on the week of the longest run in the training—the twenty-mile run—and I had to figure out how to fit it in the week before leaving, without my running partner who was running it in the city with our church team while I was gone. I enlisted the help of my amazing

Respect the mile
you are in in your
life right now.

assistant Tricia, who thankfully rode her bike alongside me to keep me company for fifteen miles of the run that day.

Through it all, I did fall in love with the small daily steps, with the process, with the conversations my neighbor and I had, with the chance to be outside in nature breathing and moving, with the feeling of finishing a run even when I felt tired or uncertain or scared. I stayed focused on the "smallness" of what I needed to do each day, instead of the "bigness" of the race. One step at a time.

In the first weeks of October, we finished the training program, and then we headed to Chicago. The race was on a cool, windy day in the city, but the sun was shining. At the starting gate, we were nervous, terrified, excited, and ready. Armed with our water bottles and energy gummies, and with our race tags carefully pinned to our orange World Vision shirts, we took off with the tens of thousands of other runners who had gathered to run the race. The energy of the crowds along the roads and of being smack-dab in the middle of that many people pursuing such a monumental achievement was electric. We had to be careful at the start of the race to not get ahead of our pace due to all of the adrenaline coursing through our bodies. The crowds lining the streets pulsated with energy. They yelled encouraging words to us, even using our names since we had them on the front of our jerseys. It felt like being carried along in the current of a river, their cheers pulling us forward.

I'm not even sure who said it first, but around mile eight, my running partner and I started saying to each other, "Respect the mile." We were simply running the eighth mile, and though we still felt gloriously excited and energized in this early part of the race, we didn't get cocky and underestimate the length of the next 18.2 miles. If we were going to finish this race, we had to respect the mile.

What do you do when you respect something? You pay attention to it. You give it undivided presence. You show up with your best for it. You listen to what it has to teach you. You don't have to like it, but you can always choose to respect it. This would be our singular mission: respect the mile.

When we saw so many of our friends and family who had rearranged their lives to come to the city to cheer for us carrying gigantic signs (one even a four-foot-tall picture of my face), noisemakers, and pom-poms, we celebrated the brief but meaningful moments we had with each of them. We gave hugs, took pictures, waved, and then we got back on the road and said to each other, "Respect the mile."

When we saw a guy who had no visible shirt or pants holding a poster board strategically at his midsection that said "Smile or I will drop my sign!" we smiled widely. And we appreciated his sense of humor (and the fact that he actually did have shorts on behind the sign), and then we said to each other, "Respect *that* mile."

When we passed through Pilsen, the hub of Chicago's Hispanic community, we saw people dancing the salsa and heard them cheering us on in Spanish, and we did a little cha-cha ourselves and said to each other, "Respect the mile."

When we ran through Boystown, several drag queens were celebrating runners by dancing on a stage bedecked with silver streamers and disco balls, and we waved and sang along with their rendition of Aretha Franklin: "R-E-S-P-E-C-T the mile!"

When we got to mile twenty-three and were legitimately too tired to talk anymore, and the novelty had worn off and our feet hurt and the crowds were more sparse and less enthusiastic, we did not think, "*Only* 3.2 more miles to go." No way. We just put one foot in front of the other, and again, this time more quietly to conserve energy, we said, "Respect

Changing your thought habits is like training for and running a marathon: it requires small daily changes.

mile twenty-three." Because in running, there is no *only*. You respect the mile you are in.

As I ran, I thought about the most difficult run of the entire training journey. It was not the 26.2 miles I ran on the day of the marathon. It was an obscure twelve-mile run I did *not* respect. You may not know this, but you only ever run twenty miles when you are training for a marathon. The twenty-mile run about ten days before the race is a really big deal with lots of hype and anticipation because the next week, the "taper" begins, and you drop down to running twelve miles, then ten, and then down to only a few miles in the days right before the race. And there is the dangerous word: *only*. Before that run, I remember thinking, "Oh, it's *only* twelve miles. No problem. I've got this." Never in all the runs had I *ever* thought *only*—until that run. But for some reason, I shifted my mindset, feeling overly confident after finishing the twenty, and that twelve-mile run was the most grueling run of the entire six months. It was hot and muggy. My legs ached, and I had a hard time controlling my breathing. Each mile felt like five. I learned that day to not overlook even one step in any run. I suffered because I did not respect the mile.

When my neighbor and I rounded the final corner to run the last 0.2 miles of the 26.2-mile marathon course, we were barely running. Our gait looked more like an exhausted shuffle, but we were still moving. The crowds close to the finish line were thick and loud, and tears streamed down our faces as we crossed the finish line. We were wrapped in foil blankets and health-care "spotters" watched us carefully in case anyone collapsed from fatigue or exhaustion. I shuffled forward through the thick crowds of fellow finishers and reflected back to the very beginning of our journey and the first miles we walked and ran when we were most decidedly *not* going to run a marathon. Each day, we respected the mile. We didn't know when we started where each mile would take us, but that respect carried us across the finish line of a life-long experience and accomplishment I will cherish forever. We had done it.

I want to challenge you with this message in a bigger sense today as you finish reading this book. Respect the mile you are in in your life right now. Respect the mile.

Maybe you started this book thinking you were just going to pick up a few tips on how to be more efficient and have more time for life outside of work. Maybe you were exhausted and wondering how much longer you could keep doing everything you do for your work and for your family at home also. Maybe you wanted to increase your influence, impact, and income—without more work. Maybe you were like me and not thinking too far ahead, like the day when I asked my friend for the marathon training schedule, wanting to simply shake up my workouts a bit. Like me, when you opened to its first page, you didn't think this book would challenge you to a massive overhaul in the way you think. You had no plans to run a marathon.

But maybe you started to make small changes as you read, adding a boundary with a domineering family member here and scheduling some more fun and guilt-free play there. Maybe you hired someone to help you with the household chores that drain you. Maybe you started to recognize the value of your own areas of genius. Maybe you started to pay attention to structures you have been resisting and then you started to identify the unhealed pain that was creating the resistance. And maybe you started to think like we did with each daily run that you really could run 26.2 miles. Maybe with each chapter, you started to believe that you could make some real changes. Maybe you realized that if you continue to change your habits of thinking, you *could* actually create more income and impact without working more hours.

One thing is certain: changing thought habits is like training for and running a marathon. It's not fast. It requires small daily shifts. Changing external behaviors alone creates fleeting results, and if just working harder were the answer, you wouldn't have picked up this book in the first place. *You simply cannot outwork your thought habits.* The change must start from within you.

Also remember that no matter what your "marathon" is, and no matter where you are in the training process, you absolutely must respect the mile you are running right now. The mile you are in right now might be a glorious, easy mile with lots of people cheering for you, promotions, financial abundance, and progress. Respect it. Or it might be a grueling, painful mile where you have lost your passion for your work, your best employee just left for another job, and you aren't sure you can cover payroll. Respect it. You could be thinking about moving on to something else, even though what you've built is so successful and most people would love to be where you are. Respect it. Or you could be experiencing astronomical growth with revenue and profits doubling every year. Respect it.

Your mile, the one you are running *right now*, has something important to say to you. Are you listening? It will keep repeating the message until you get it. Respect it. Be in it fully. You will need what this mile has to teach you down the road, even if it's the worst mile of your life. The finish line is ahead, and it is important, but so is the journey, so is the mile you are running right now. So . . .

Respect the mile.

Respect the mile.

Respect the mile.

Acknowledgments

R YAN, AVERY, Anthony, and Andrew—Our family and my love for each of you is the driving force behind everything I do, including the creation of this book. #kempnation is and always will be my number one priority. I hope someday you all read my words and know that you inspired me to write them.

My parents and mother-in-law—In the lotto of life, I hit the jackpot having you as my parents and you, Sue, as my mother-in-law. Every step of this writing and publishing process has been covered in your unwavering encouragement and belief in me, just as every other endeavor I have undertaken has been. Ryan and I strive every day to be the kind of committed, loving parents to our children that you all have been to us.

AJ Harper—Your Top Three Book Workshop gave me both a safe and encouraging community and the structure and tools I needed to make a lifelong dream of writing a book a reality. Thank you for teaching me that as you so eloquently wrote in *Write a Must-Read*, "A book is not about something. A book is for someone. It's not about your topic; it's for the people you serve and the people you hope to serve." And all of the writers in the world together say, "Amen."

Sarah Hemenover at Sarah Jane Photography—Thank you for using your artistic genius and discerning eye to create the picture of me on the cover of this book. You captured my spirit, not just my physical being with your camera.

My support team—A special thanks especially to my office assistant Tricia and my business manager Jen. Thank you for being my sounding boards, my voice of reason that reins me in, and my biggest supporters. You see me at my worst and at my best, and you are steadily there through it all.

My coaches—Throughout my career, I have worked with some of the best business coaches in the world. Each of you impacted me, taught me, listened to me, and helped me grow by continuously giving me a safe space to process my thoughts and feelings. Thank you.

Page Two Publishing—Big thank-yous go out to Trena White for understanding my book even better than I did upon reading the manuscript. In our first conversation, you said, "This feels like a book *all* women should read, not only those who lead." And so it is. Thank you for creating and leading the team that continuously brings books of great value into the world. Emily Schultz, my editor. Working with you to craft these words into the final draft felt like a long walk and meaningful conversation with a good friend. I enjoyed our work together so much, I was sad when it ended. Louise Hill and Beate Schwirtlich, my project managers, thank you for all of the patient reminders, managing all of the details, and steering the ship all the way to our destination! Thank you for the cover and interior design work, Taysia Louie. The book is simply stunning. Finally, to Rachel Ironstone, the copy editor extraordinaire who put even a former English teacher like me to shame with her impeccable grasp of the English language, its punctuation, and vast complexity. And for the final round of proofreading and catching every last error that my eyes skipped over after countless reads, Crissy Boylan, thank you. You were the finishing touch the book needed.

To the authors of every book I've ever read (and there are so, so many)—The experience of bringing this book into the world has given me a deep appreciation for your courage, tenacity, and brilliance. Thank you for your words and for putting them into the world in the form of a book. A piece of each and every one of you is in these pages.

Notes

2: Leverage the Value of Your Natural Genius

"What feels like fun to me": James Clear, *Atomic Habits: An Easy &
Proven Way to Build Good Habits & Break Bad Ones* (New York:
Penguin Random House, 2018).

Here are a few more questions: Clear, *Atomic Habits.*

"In my work, what produces": Gay Hendricks, *The Big Leap: Conquer
Your Hidden Fear and Take Life to the Next Level* (New York:
HarperOne, 2009).

"She looked at our prices and": "Brené with Priya Parker on *The Art of
Gathering*," *Unlocking Us with Brené Brown* podcast, November 25,
2020, https://brenebrown.com/podcast/brene-with-priya-parker-
on-the-art-of-gathering/.

3: Stop Giving So Much

Heath describes proudly sitting down: Byron Heath, "This realization
I had [...] WE'RE STILL ROOTING FOR YOU!" Facebook, July 27,
2021, https://www.facebook.com/photo/?fbid=1010379898718
7954&set=a.835107058534.

"And the tree was happy": Shel Silverstein, *The Giving Tree* (New York:
Harper & Row, 1964).

"And as each generation played": Topher Payne, *The Tree Who Set
Healthy Boundaries*, https://www.topherpayne.com/giving-tree.

4: You Don't Have to Work More

concept of "scheduled guilt-free play": Neil Fiore, *The Now Habit:
A Strategic Program for Overcoming Procrastination and Enjoying
Guilt-Free Play* (New York: TarcherPerigee, 2007), 80–81.

"This can happen when you": Fiore, *The Now Habit*, 92.

James Clear imagines their conversation: James Clear, "The Ivy Lee Method: The Daily Routine Experts Recommend for Peak Productivity," James Clear, https://jamesclear.com/ivy-lee.

5: Can I Get a Little Woo-Woo?

"Move your hand in haste before": Og Mandino, *The Greatest Salesman in the World* (New York: Bantam Books, 1968), 98.

The video starts with an interview: Fox Family Entertainment, "The Greatest Showman | 'This Is Me' with Keala Settle | 20th Century FOX," YouTube, December 24, 2017, https://youtu.be/XLFEVHWD_NE.

"The subconscious mind is everyone's": Tom McCarthy, *The Breakthrough Code: A Story about Living a Life without Limits* (Monee, IL: Shining Icon, 2022).

6: Boundaries Protect You and Allow You to Grow

"We know that 95 percent": Dave Blanchard, *Today I Begin a New Life* (United States: OgPress, 2012).

"Those privileges and that power": Melissa Urban, *The Book of Boundaries: Set the Limits That Will Set You Free* (New York: The Dial Press, 2022).

"making clear what's okay and": Brené Brown, *Dare to Lead: Brave Work. Tough Conversations. Whole Hearts.* (New York: Random House, 2018).

"clear limits you establish around": Urban, *The Book of Boundaries*.

"boundaries are the gateway to": Nedra Glover Tawwab, *Set Boundaries, Find Peace: A Guide to Reclaiming Yourself* (New York: Tarcher Perigee, 2021).

"Boundaries define us": Henry Cloud and John Townsend, *Boundaries: When to Say Yes, How to Say No to Take Control of Your Life* (Grand Rapids, MI: Zondervan, 2002).

"boundaries are the distance": Prentis Hemphill, @prentishemphill, "Boundaries Are the Distance," Instagram, April 5, 2021.

Plett uses a picture of a cell: Heather Plett, *The Art of Holding Space: A Practice of Love, Liberation, and Leadership* (Vancouver, BC: Page Two, 2020).

7: This Is Where I End and You Begin

"If you feel tired, fatigued or burned out": Alan Cohen, *A Course in Miracles Made Easy: Mastering the Journey from Fear to Love* (Carlsbad, CA: Hay House, Inc., 2015).

setting boundaries happens in two parts: Glennon Doyle, "Dr. Brené Brown: On Holding Boundaries & Facing Our Fear," *We Can Do Hard Things*, December 2, 2021, https://www.audible.ca/pd /Dr-Bren%C3%A9-Brown-On-Holding-Boundaries-Facing-Our-Fear-Podcast/B09MVQJF5G?ref=a_pd_We-Can_c1_lAsin_6_1.

8: Money Is a Mirror

the belief that "money equals security": Kyle Cease, *The Illusion of Money: Why Chasing Money Is Stopping You from Receiving It* (Carlsbad, CA: Hay House, Inc., 2019).

"Seeing money as your only source": Cease, *The Illusion of Money.*

"Money is a renewable resource": Jen Sincero, *You Are a Badass at Making Money: Master the Mindset of Wealth* (New York: Viking, 2017).

9: Do a Thorough Check of Your Environment

"work performed in the home": Melinda Gates, *The Moment of Lift: How Empowering Women Changes the World* (New York: Flatiron Books, 2019).

telling numbers about the current makeup: US Bureau of Labor Statistics, "Labor Force Participation Rate for Women Highest in the District of Columbia in 2022," *TED: The Economics Daily*, March 7, 2023, https://www.bls.gov/opub/ted/2023/labor-force -participation-rate-for-women-highest-in-the-district-of-columbia -in-2022.htm.

"On average, women do seven": Gates, *The Moment of Lift.*

a theory in law enforcement called: Staff, "Broken Windows Theory," *Psychology Today*, https://www.psychologytoday.com/us/basics/ broken-windows-theory.

10: Surrender to Structure

"I will persist until I succeed": Mandino, *The Greatest Salesman.*

"If I don't write every day": Stephen King, *On Writing: A Memoir of the Craft* (New York: Hodder & Stoughton, 2012).

a study done at the University of California: Kristen Wong, "How Long It Takes to Get Back on Track After a Distraction," *LifeHacker*, July 29, 2015, https://lifehacker.com/how-long-it-takes-to-get-back-on-track-after-a-distract-1720708353.

"What you are about to do is the foundation": Mike Michalowicz, *Profit First: Transform Your Business from a Cash-Eating Monster to a Money-Making Machine* (New York: Portfolio/Penguin, 2017).

"giant, scary, soul-sucking, cash-eating monsters": Michalowicz, *Profit First*, 11.

Your To-Do List

M Y HOPE IS that reading this book felt like a one-on-one coaching session with me—an exploration of where you are and where you want to be. At the end of each coaching session I do with my clients, I send them a to-do list based on what we covered in our conversation. So, as an exclamation point to our session together, here is yours:

1 **Follow Me**

I love to connect with people through social media.

 @amykempinc
 Amy Kemp

2 **Sign Up for my Monthly Newsletter**

AmyKemp.com/newsletter

3 **Take Your Next Step with Amy Kemp, Inc.**

- Register for my next webinar or work through one in my collection: AmyKemp.com/resources

- Join my next round of Encounter groups: AmyKemp.com/services

- Inquire about my one-on-one coaching experience called Empower: AmyKemp.com/empower

About the Author

AMY KEMP is the owner and CEO of Amy Kemp, Inc. She uses over twenty years of experience growing her own successful business in sales to guide her work and to authentically connect with leaders and business professionals within her growing company. The purpose of Amy's work is simple: she helps leaders and business professionals understand how deeply habits of thinking affect every part of their work and lives.

Amy has led hundreds of women in a four-month small group coaching engagement called Encounter, and she has also worked with hundreds of leaders in her one-on-one coaching experience called Empower. In addition, she partners with leaders as they develop their teams at both large and small companies.

In her webinars and in-person workshops, Amy is an effective communicator who is best known for making complicated concepts simple and accessible to all people. Amy's clients and audiences feel understood and affirmed and also challenged to become more.

Amy lives in the Chicagoland area with her husband, Ryan, and their three children. You can learn more about her work at AmyKemp.com.

Made in the USA
Monee, IL
17 February 2024

53651587R00152